Legal Rainmaking Myths:
What You Think You Know About
Business Development Can Kill Your Practice
By Julie A. Fleming, J.D.

Published by:
Crow Creek Press
Atlanta, GA

ISBN 978-0-9911251-2-8

Printed in the United States of America

Legal Rainmaking Myths:

What You Think You Know About Business Development Can Kill Your Practice

Julie A. Fleming

Julie A. Fleming, J.D.

Atlanta, Georgia

Table of Contents

Dedication

To SHF and JDF,

without whom nothing would be possible.

Acknowledgments

I am grateful for the support, encouragement, and wisdom offered by so many dear friends and mentors.

My clients and former colleagues: thank you for sharing your experiences and struggles and for prompting me to catalog your breakthroughs. Your honesty and courage is remarkable. I am honored to work with such fine lawyers and delightful people.

My mentors Suzanne Evans and Larry Winget, along with their entire team: thank you for your teaching and your candid feedback. You tell it like it is, and you have inspired me to grow both personally and professionally. Here's to making the decision right, every single day.

My editor Renée Barnow: thank you for your invaluable contributions. This book is far better for your input. I appreciate your support and friendship more than I could ever tell you.

My dear friend and business manager Vicky Likens: thank you for believing in me and my work even when I didn't. I am grateful for you each and every day.

My father J.D. Fleming, Jr.: thank you for teaching me about the practice of law by example and for demonstrating that business development isn't just about what you *do*, it's about who you *are*.

Online Resources

Please visit <u>LegalRainmakingMyths.com</u> to access additional resources for use with *Legal Rainmaking Myths: What You Think You Know About Business Development Can Kill Your Practice.* Resources include the Law Practice Profitability Audit, a free assessment that will pinpoint where you are in your business development efforts and whether you are a Rainmaker, a Mistmaker, or a Drylander. The audit will also help you to identify some of the rainmaking myths you may have accepted as true. After you've completed the audit, you'll receive a personalized report that will set out next steps specific to your needs, along with follow-up resources designed to give you simple, bite-sized actions that you can implement immediately.

A word about client stories

Because client confidentiality is paramount in all consulting and coaching engagement, the stories included herein represent composite clients, with names and other identifying details changed.

Preface

The success of every private practice law firm, whether a sole practitioner or a mega-firm, depends on that firm having enough clients to cover expenses and bring in a profit. In years past, not every lawyer in a firm was required to bring in new business. Technicians were highly prized, business was plentiful (or plentiful enough), and firms prospered with a handful of lawyers who were able to land the lion's share of billable work.

More recently, however, business development has become a central focus of law practice management. New business is required to keep sole practices afloat, and lawyers in larger firms generally acknowledge that professional advancement (and even survival) depends on their ability to carry their own weight, at least after the first few years in practice.

Thanks to this focus, lawyers seek out information about marketing, how to bring in new business, and how to retain and expand client engagements. Few law schools offer any training in business acquisition, so lawyers rely on mentors, training, and written information. Books, articles, and workshops about how to become a rainmaker are readily available. Lawyers consume this information but too often fail to achieve the success they seek with the speed they desire.

After years working as a lawyer in private practice at both small and large firms, I began consulting with lawyers in 2006. Only then did I notice that a client's level of motivation did not predict success in business development. Time and again lawyers would tell me that they were determined to build a book of business, and too often I watched them stumble, decide that perhaps they weren't cut out to be rainmakers, and sometimes even leave practice rather than keep plugging away—even when, objectively, every indicator would suggest that they could build a consistent pipeline of business sufficient to support a practice. Sometimes we would break through the block, but other times the lawyers would simply melt away, ashamed and hopeless.

And then, I met Drew and discovered not only what the block is, but also how to smash it. During our first conversation, Drew told me that he'd done everything he could think of to build his practice, but he hadn't been successful. His partner, with a similar practice, had brought in enough business to support the firm and encouraged Drew to try the tactics that had worked so well for her. Drew tried, but didn't land anything close to enough business to support even his own practice. He was discouraged and felt guilty, with his partner's resentment threatening the firm.

Even though we worked out a step-by-step business development plan, Drew came to each of our meetings having accomplished nothing. He wanted to have a vibrant practice and to contribute to the firm's growth, yet he couldn't find a way to break through whatever was holding him back. Finally, I asked Drew what he believed to be true about business development. He told me he believed if he were a good enough lawyer, clients would seek him out, eliminating the need to market. He shared his fear that asking for business would always come across as pushy and that it might even be unethical. And even when he received a referral, his desire not to bother anyone prevented him from following through. Every time Drew made a statement I would ask why, and we would uncover another layer of worry, fear, or misconception. We both came to understand that what he *thought* he knew about business development was killing his practice. As we examined these beliefs, Drew began to recognize their fallacy, and he was able to take a new and more effective approach to business development. As he put new habits into place, he began to build a book of business.

I began to make similar inquiries of other unsuccessful would-be legal rainmakers and discovered that Drew was not alone. Almost every time I asked *why*, a fallacy was uncovered. And that's when I realized that lawyers who fail at business development have accepted as true myths about how and whether to engage in rainmaking activity. The myths usually center on the necessity or urgency for taking on business development activity, on the mechanics of that activity, or on the beliefs that surround the activity or the idea of working to get new clients. As a result, they touch on every aspects of business development, from the need for rainmaking activity to the professionalism and ethics of such activity.

These myths typically go unexamined. They color what lawyers believe they can and should do, and they shadow lawyers' perceptions about their own success. Similar to a house built on a faulty foundation, a business development plan that rests on myths will produce a solid book of business sluggishly if at all.

As lawyers, we are fact driven. We go for the truth and seek to expose falsehood. This approach benefits us when it comes to debunking myths.

When the myths are exposed and the truth is revealed, lawyers are able to see clearly how to approach marketing and business development and are able to implement the necessary steps to build a book of business confidently and fruitfully.

And what about those lawyers who don't see myths for what they are? They may find some success, perhaps even significant short-term success, but their practices will never reach full potential because those lawyers are operating according to rules that are outdated or simply false.

Uncovering the myths and realities of legal business development demolishes rainmaking blocks and paves the way to a practice that is financially successful, professionally satisfying, and personally meaningful.

After close to fifteen years in private practice, launching and growing my own business, and consulting with lawyers through the height of the Great Recession, I've come to understand the realities of rainmaking. My heart breaks every time I talk with a lawyer who confides that she feels stuck because she's never been able to develop business or who tells me that he left practice because he just couldn't get enough clients to survive. I believe that the vast majority of lawyers are good people who seek to serve clients who need them. When lawyers figure out business development, they have stronger practices, they represent their clients more effectively, they contribute to their families and the causes they support, and they have successful, professionally satisfying, and personally meaningful lives. Helping lawyers to reach that point is why I get out of bed every morning, and why I wrote this book.

Julie A. Fleming
Atlanta, Georgia
May 2013

How to Use this Book

This book is divided into three parts.

Part I—Rainmaking Demystified (and De-Mythified) builds the case that rainmaking myths undermine lawyers' ability to succeed with business development. Chapter 1, "What You Think You Know About Business Development is Wrong," explains how I discovered the existence of rainmaking myths and how I realized that myths are at the core of the rainmaker's dilemma. Chapter 2, "Solving the Rainmaker's Dilemma," describes how recognizing the four categories of rainmaking myths offers lawyers an exit from the cycle of business development failure.

Part II—NUMB: Myths that Undermine Would-Be Rainmakers explores each of the four categories of myths that leave lawyers numb to business development and debunks the most prevalent myths in each of the four categories. You can dip in and read about the myths that resonate with you or read sequentially, as you prefer. Either way, be sure to keep notes when you find a myth that strikes close to home.

Part III—Rainmaking Strategies & Tactics: A Primer provides an overview of how to engage in business development activity. The section is neither all-inclusive nor exhaustive. Instead, you will find a high-level overview of rainmaking strategy and tactics and easy-to-implement suggestions to help you advance your business development efforts.

Finally, be sure to visit LegalRainmakingMyths.com to download additional resources and to take the Law Practice Profitability Audit.

Introduction

Here's the truth:

- The days of having a practice supported by being a "great lawyer" are gone forever.

- In today's economy, every successful private practice lawyer is a rainmaker who has created an effective plan for building a consistent pipeline of new business.

- Every lawyer can and must learn to bring in enough business to support a practice and make a profit.

- Building a book of business requires mastering a set of business development skills and attitudes and investing time and resources.

- There is no single way to develop business. Every lawyer must know how best to use his or her own skills.

- Rainmaking success depends on having a well-designed plan and executing it persistently and consistently.

A darker truth lurks beneath the surface of countless business development attempts: lawyers have bought into numerous myths about rainmaking. These myths tend to go unexamined. They are perpetuated as part of the culture of legal practice. Rainmaking myths undermine believers' ability to develop business, and they kill practices as a result.

The New Legal Economy Demands that Lawyers Be Rainmakers

Despite a few market blips, the legal industry grew rapidly between the 1970s and the early 2000s. The overall growth was strong, and the horizon for lawyers and law firms seemed almost limitless. The following statistics tell the story:

- The number of jobs available for lawyers doubled between 1970 and 2000.[1]

- Growth in lawyer ranks as of 2007 was constrained by the output of U.S. law schools.[2]

---

[1] Harvard Law School, Analysis of the Legal Profession and Law Firms (as of 2007), online at http://www.law.harvard.edu/programs/plp/pages/statistics.php.
[2] *Id.*

- The AmLaw 100 experienced a 7.2% growth rate between 1997 and 2006.[3]

- Law office revenues grew at a 7% rate between 1998 and 2003, with 2003 profit rates of 40%.[4]

- Between 2004 and 2007, law firm revenue grew by nearly 40%, demand for services was up more than 10%, realization grew slightly, and profits per partner increased by almost 25%.[5]

In 2008, however, the legal market (and the global economy) hit meltdown. The subprime mortgage crisis kicked off a cascade of crises that quickly affected the legal market as well.

- From 2007 to 2010, law firm revenue decreased by about 3%, demand decreased by almost 10%, realization dropped by about 7%, and profits per partner increased by less than 10%.[6]

---

[3] *Id.*

[4] *Id.*

[5] *Hildebrandt/Citi Private Bank 2012 Client Advisory,* available at https://peermonitor.thomsonreuters.com/ThomsonPeer/docs/2012_Client_Advisory.pdf

[6] *Id.*

- In 2009 alone, the legal industry decreased by at least 12,219 jobs, of which 4,656 were attorney positions.[7]

- Between 2008 and 2012, an aggregate of at least 16,204 legal positions were eliminated, of which 6,162 were attorney positions.[8]

The legal world has changed, and it's unlikely that we will return to the world that existed before 2008. What had appeared early in the decade to be an exciting new era was, in fact, an unsustainable boom brought to a close by a faltering economy, legal document providers and low-cost legal services that harness technology and divert clients from traditional practices, and a shift in the balance of strength between clients and their attorneys.

Although the economy began a slow recovery in 2011 and 2012, the legal economy has lagged behind. Here is a summary today's world:

- Law firm profits grew by 4.3% in 2012, but that increase was due primarily to non-sustainable factors such as increased collections and a moderate growth in expenses.[9]

---

[7] http://lawshucks.com/layoff-tracker/#ytd-chart
[8] http://lawshucks.com/layoff-tracker/#ytd-chartId.
[9] *Citi: Firms Posted 4.3 Percent Rise in 2012 Profits*, available at http://www.americanlawyer.com/PubArticleALD.jsp?id=1202587253629&thepage=1

- Average billable hours per lawyer dropped from 2011 to 2012, a mark of concern in the midst of economic recovery.[10]

- Legal sector employment grew at only half the rate of the overall workforce in 2012.[11]

This new reality, though harsh, also offers new opportunity. Individual attorneys now have the ability to build the practice they want. In the old days, lawyers could expect to join a firm (or start a practice) and feel the security that comes with the expectation of lifelong employment. The trend favoring lateral moves has been in play for over a decade, and the layoffs in 2008-2010 put a final end to that sense of security. Each lawyer is now responsible for creating her own professional security by building a book of business that is portable should the lawyer choose (or be forced) to change firms. Having a portable book of business, and the knowledge and skill required to build it, means never having to worry about job security again.

Unlike decades past, simply being employed by a law firm is no guarantee of security. Not only have firms laid off unproductive lawyers (both associates and partners) to reduce overhead and protect profits per partner, but law firm mergers and collapses have left many good attorneys scrambling for work. Even as the economic recovery seems to be continuing as of this mid-2013

---

[10] *Id.*
[11] *Job Growth in Legal Services Lagged Behind National Rate in 2012*, available at http://www.americanlawyer.com/PubArticleALD.jsp?germane=1202586718537&id=1202585060375

writing, data shows that mergers are on the increase[12] and additional law firm failures appear inevitable.[13] Rainmakers are assets for law firm mergers, and they are often able to jump to a new firm if they discover signs of financial trouble in their current firm, frequently hastening that firm's demise. Without a book of business, professional security is illusory.

Statistics show that as a group lawyers are not happy professionals. Some 50% of lawyers surveyed state that they might not or would not become lawyers again if given the choice, and 30-40% of those would leave practice but for the golden handcuffs they perceive to hold them in place.[14] Lawyers who build their own book of business get to choose what kind of law they practice and what kinds of clients they want to represent. They can decide how much they want to work and earn, and they can set up (or join) a practice that supports those goals. As a result, they find not only increased professional security but also heightened professional satisfaction.

---

[12] *Law Firm Merger Activity Up in 2013, Report Says,* available at http://www.americanlawyer.com/PubArticleALD.jsp?id= 1202594853322&Law_Firm_Merger_Activity_Up_in_2013_Report_Says

[13] *See* https://www.youtube.com/watch?v=R5b8AclrZuE&feature=youtu.be; http://www.legalweek.com/legal-week/analysis/2243680/partners-predict-further-law-firm-failures-as-recent-collapses-shake-confidence

[14] *See* http://www.abajournal.com/magazine/article/pulse_of_the_legal_profession; http://www.psychologytoday.com/blog/therapy-matters/201105/the-depressed-lawyer; http://www.lawyerswithdepression.com/articles/why-are-lawyers-so-unhappy/ (excerpting the chapter "Why Are Lawyers So Unhappy?" from Martin Seligman, Ph.D.'s *Authentic Happiness: Using the New Positive Psychology to Realize Your Potential for Lasting Fulfillment*).

The bottom line? Every private practice lawyer must be able to bring in at least enough business to support his practice and make a profit. While the news may come to some as a rude awakening (after all, law schools rarely mention client acquisition and often only touch on client service), lawyers should regard it as a positive. When you can land business, your practice and your professional future are secure.

Part I

Rainmaking Demystified (and De-Mythified)

Chapter 1

What You Think You Know About Business Development Is Wrong

Late novelist David Foster Wallace shared this anecdote, which aptly describes the situation many lawyers face, in a 2005 commencement speech at Kenyon College:

> There are these two young fish swimming along, and they happen to meet an older fish swimming the other way, who nods at them and says, "Morning, boys, how's the water?" And the two young fish swim on for a bit, and then eventually one of them looks over at the other and says, "What the hell is water?"

As lawyers, we're swimming in a sea of misinformation and inaccurate thinking about rainmaking. While no book could capture all of the myths, I've corralled some of the most prevalent ones. In some cases, simply identifying them is enough to dispel them; in others, the truth must be amplified before the myth can be fully debunked.

Like most law students, I jumped into the proverbial fishbowl, never realizing that I was choosing unfiltered water. Looking back, I recognize that I accepted certain myths as truth. Although the myths developed over time (beginning as early as law school, when the lack of any discussion about client acquisition led me to believe that being a good lawyer would be enough to make clients seek me out), it wasn't until the myths were shattered that I even discovered their existence. While my own story differs in details from others' experiences, the process of accepting and then uncovering myths about business development tends to follow a pattern.

Law Student and Junior Law Firm Associate Myths

Before I entered law school, I talked with my father, a longtime partner and leader in a large firm based in Atlanta and Washington, D.C., about various aspects of practice. Rainmaking was never a topic of those conversations. I knew that he had clients, of course, and I had observed that he entertained clients and came to regard many of them as friends. I never thought to ask how he found those clients or how they found him, and he never raised the topic. My assumption (to the extent that I ever even considered the question) was that affiliating with an excellent firm and skilled colleagues and then doing good work would be enough to become a sought-after practitioner.

Law school never addressed business development or how a lawyer should expect to acquire clients, except to discuss ethical prohibitions against solicitation. I learned that attorney advertising was forbidden until the 1977 case *Bates v. State Bar of Arizona,*[15] and I came to understand that even if permissible under the rules, advertising and solicitation could hardly be considered professional. Like most of my classmates, I did not expect to start my own practice. I accepted the premise shared explicitly and implicitly that success as a lawyer meant working in a large law firm, and I felt fully justified in expecting that someone else would provide the clients I would serve.

After law school, I took a few detours, first clerking for a federal judge and then working for a sole practitioner while I returned to school to get a biology degree so that I could sit for the patent bar. When it became clear to me that the sole practitioner didn't have a reliable stream of clients, I looked for a new job and quickly moved to the Atlanta office of an international mega-firm.

M
Y
T
H

Notice the myth: Someone else is responsible for bringing in business. There's no need and no urgency for me to acquire new business.

---

[15]   433 U.S. 350 (1977).

I focused my practice on patent litigation, which meant that most of the matters I worked on were valued in the tens or hundreds of millions of dollars—and that they demanded hours and hours of work. I kept my head down and plowed away, giving thought to business development only occasionally. Aware, of course, that billable work had to come from somewhere, I read articles about business development when I happened to see them. I even concluded that at some indefinite point in the future, I would need to bring in some business. Mostly, though, I accepted the firm's unspoken message that my role was to do the work that others secured and that my success would lie in my performance.

M
Y   *Notice the myth: If you're a good enough lawyer, you*
T   *need not worry about bringing in new business. Good*
H   *lawyers do not need to work at business development.*

To my pleasant surprise, the firm did provide business development training for the associates when I was in my fourth year there: a single lunch'n'learn. Several of the more successful partners shared how they obtained their clients. These partners told the associates to meet people, to write, and to speak, and the implication was that clients would find us as a result. The partners spoke with a clear undertone: being a lawyer of a certain caliber means that you need not, and in fact should not, seek out or ask for business. No one suggested that we view business development as a priority, much less an urgency. In fact, the point of the training seemed to be that landing business is a long-term proposition best left to partners.

M Y T H

Notice the myths: Business development comprises certain activities that will make new business find you. You need not ask for business, and doing so is distasteful. Business development consists of some acceptable activities and some unacceptable ones. (These myths address both the mechanics of rainmaking and the beliefs that underlie business development activity.)

After the meeting, I asked a few fellow associates what their plans were, and theirs mirrored my own: get back to work. Build some relationships with clients, but focus primarily on cranking out briefs, preparing for and handling depositions, drafting memoranda and more memoranda. After all, with so many hours of work lined up, why should we spend time trying to bring in more? We were still fairly junior and the matters we were handling were so highly valued, so none of us believed we could actually win new business. At some fuzzy level, I was aware that I would need to learn how to get business at some point, but the lunch'n'learn training—and the seeming lack of interest when I approached the partner I worked for to discuss beginning business development efforts—left me convinced that I was correct to view rainmaking as a process that I would learn over a period of years and that I need not be concerned about getting new business yet.

M
Y   *Notice the myths: When there's enough work to do,*
T   *there's no need to focus on business development.*
        Junior lawyers have no role in business development.
H   *If there's no urgency to get more work, there's no*
        urgency to engage in business development.

By 2004, I had worked at the megafirm for five years. I was feeling restless: my goal had been to focus on patent litigation related to the life sciences, but all of my cases addressed technology related to electrical engineering, physical chemistry, and software. I had never wanted to spend my time looking at massive stacks of patents that described the flow of electrons, but that was the work available. And then even that work slowed down. I was concerned that I might not have enough work to do, and I felt rising alarm as I saw my task list—and worse yet, my timesheet—shrink. Colleagues on my team started working for other partners.

One day, while taking a break from reading yet another patent about electronics, I became fully aware that not only was I stuck doing work that I didn't particularly want to do, but that even that work seemed to be drying up. Stuck and bored was not what I'd envisioned for my career. As I had years earlier while working for the sole practitioner, I decided to move to another firm. My timing was impeccable: a few months later I was told that my advancement within the firm was at an end, and that although I didn't need to hurry, I would need to pursue other employment.

M
Y
T
H
Notice the myth: If you don't have enough work, or if you don't enjoy the work you're doing, your best option is to move to another law firm that has more business and, you hope, work you will like. Avoid the need for business development as long as possible.

The Myths Shatter—Business Development Becomes Urgent and Important: Now What?

I reached out to one of the recruiters who had been calling me over the years, and our meeting started well. The economy was strong in 2004, and plenty of jobs were available in my field. Toward the end of our conversation, however, he raised a topic I hadn't expected: my book of business.

Recruiter Richard and I were sitting at a round table in a small office. He'd been leaning toward me and talking animatedly. "Tell me," he said almost casually, "about your book of business. What's your client load like?"

I tried not to show my surprise—after all, Richard was an experienced recruiter, so surely he would understand that a fifth-year associate working on cases valued in the hundreds of millions of dollars would not be expected to have a book of business yet. When I told him that I didn't have clients of my own, he leaned back in his chair. He almost gasped, "Really?" With my confirmation, he removed his glasses and began to rub his temples. As I watched with growing uneasiness, reeling at the shift in the conversation, he sighed, put his glasses back on, and said, "Well, I'll do what I can for you."

Our conversation ended a few minutes later, as he hurried me out of his office. What had been a pleasant, encouraging chat had turned troubling. I was surprised that a veteran recruiter would be so misinformed about what to expect from young associates. Nevertheless, I had a list of recruiters that other lawyers suggested I contact, and I made appointments with several of them.

To my surprise, then my shock, then my horror, each subsequent conversation proceeded in the same way. Encouraging comments about my background and the ease with which I'd find a new position, followed by what I came to consider the Dreaded Question about clients, ending quickly with sighs and weak promises to be in touch.

After having several of those conversations, I sat in my car and wondered... Is it possible that I was mistaken? Had I somehow overlooked a critical aspect of my own career development? Was it not enough to have great credentials and strong skills? If business development is so important, why was it never mentioned in law school? Why was it treated so casually by the law firm? What would it take for me to find another job?

Fortunately, I quickly landed a new position in another city, where my then-husband had just accepted a job. Sharing the firm's expectation that I'd be made partner within a year or two, I brought fresh determination to learn business development and build my own book of business. I swore that I would never again be blindsided by a question about my clientele.

Over the next few months, I learned a tremendous amount about how to bring in new work. Having realized that most of my previous beliefs about business development were inaccurate, I questioned everything I thought I knew.

For example, one belief that I identified as a myth is that there's only one way to be a rainmaker. As an introvert, I thought I knew that I needed to find a way to enjoy attending large events and meeting strangers because that's what the rainmakers I had observed seemed to do. As I talked with other lawyers and skilled non-lawyer rainmakers, I began to realize that I could use some of the activities I enjoyed to develop a clientele. One of my primary activities was (and remains today) working in the American Bar Association's Section of Science and Technology Law, where over the course of a decade I've served as one of twelve members of the Section's governing Council, as Editor-in-Chief of *The SciTech Lawyer*, the Section's flagship publication, and as an officer. Through those positions and other activity within and outside the Section, I built a vibrant network of colleagues and client contacts. I didn't yet have clients, but I began to make and receive referrals through that network and to attract new relationships as a result of the writing and speaking I did about topics related to my practice.

M	*Notice the myths: There's only one way to develop*
Y	*business. Rainmakers must be extroverts. The mechanics*
	of business development are one-size-fits-all: do not
T	*expect to find an approach that fits you, but do expect to*
H	*mold yourself to fit the successful approach.*

A Crash Course in Business Development (and a Crash) Reveals the Full Truth

While working at the new firm, I was able to rely on colleagues to bring in work while I was learning how to become a rainmaker. Not long after joining the firm, however, I left for what I then viewed as a sabbatical to work in a family business. During that time, after long conversations with former colleagues, I launched my consulting business. No longer able to stay busy and well-paid as a result of someone else's ability to bring in clients, I felt a new urgency to master business development skills, and I embarked on a crash-course education in marketing.

After a few years of hard work, I had more than replaced my law firm salary. More importantly, I had come to understand what it takes to build a book of business and a client pipeline, and I'd dispelled the myths that I had accepted as true. Initially I had resisted working on legal business development, but in 2009, I had two epiphanies:

1. The only security that exists in the practice of law (or any other business) comes through the ability to bring in enough business to support a practice.

2. Business development myths create reluctant and ineffective rainmakers.

One Thursday in early 2009, I had a full day of client appointments scheduled. During that long and painful day, every single client told me that they had been laid off or they had realistic fears that they soon would be laid off. Eager to find some way to help my clients (and, not incidentally, to save my own business), I spent the evening thinking about what would allow one lawyer to prosper in a recession while others might only survive, if that. The answer was clear, and the next day I roughed out a manifesto with the following points:

- The ONLY security that exists in the practice of law comes from your ability to bring in the business you need to support your practice.

- Being a great lawyer isn't enough to support a practice.

- At its base, practice is about serving clients, and those clients have to come from somewhere.

- If you allow yourself to believe that someone else will feed your business for the duration of your career, you are at high risk.

- If you don't have a book of business, you may be unable to move or advance within your firm, to move to a new position with another firm, or even to keep your job.

- You must engage in business activity, starting right now. The best time to embark on the path to becoming a rainmaker is as soon as you decide to enter law school. The second best time is today.

- If you are waiting for someone to offer to teach you or mentor you in business development you're waiting for something that most likely will never happen. You must seek out the help you need.

- Every lawyer can and must discover how to harness their unique strengths and opportunities to build a book of business. There is no single right way to become a rainmaker.

Armed with those truths, I began to focus my consulting more narrowly on rainmaking. Because I recognized that most lawyers operate in the same system of half-truth and uncertainty about business development that I'd inhabited, in 2009 I wrote my first book *The Reluctant Rainmaker: A Guide for Lawyers Who Hate Selling*.

The book, which became an Amazon best seller in Law Office Education, presents a step-by-step process to help lawyers bring in new business. Many of my clients implemented these principles and thrived through the recession because they were able to bring in business.

Meet Kathryn

Kathryn was a sole practitioner. Her practice yielded decent revenue, but she found that she was working harder and harder to maintain that income. During our first conversation, she told me that she wanted to work on a smaller number of higher value matters so that she wouldn't have to manage as many matters at one time. After she created a business development plan using the steps covered in *The Reluctant Rainmaker* and outlined in Part III of this book, Kathryn understood clearly how to reach the kinds of clients she wanted, and she began to work her plan consistently. Although her income took a short-term hit when she quit accepting the smaller matters, as she began moving in new professional circles and began getting more of the cases and clients she wanted, her income took off and doubled over the course of about a year.

Meet Lee

Lee was a partner in a 10-person firm (four partners, six associates). He hired me in 2007 because his book of business was much smaller than the other partners' and he felt pressured to carry his financial weight. As Kathryn and I had done, Lee and I designed a plan that would elevate his professional profile and put him in contact with more potential clients and referral sources. But Lee didn't work that plan. Instead, he came to our calls with reasons why the plan needed to be re-evaluated and excuses about why he hadn't even attempted the actions he'd promised to undertake. Although I pressed and questioned what was happening, Lee would throw up a roadblock by saying, "That's just the way I am," or "That's just how it works." After a few meetings, I told Lee that I couldn't help him if he remained unwilling to do the work, and he vanished.

The Rainmaker's Dilemma Revealed

For quite some time, my experience with Lee haunted me. He, and a few other clients (like Drew, whose story is recounted in the Preface), seemed to have a block that stopped them from implementing the steps that other lawyers were taking successfully, and I puzzled over the cause. As I talked with other lawyers and reflected on my own experiences, I began to recognize the crux of the rainmaker's dilemma.

Lawyers can easily find books and training programs to teach them how to build a book of business. They can hire coaches and consultants who will provide all the necessary "how to" information. And most lawyers in private practice are aware of the importance of business development—though some confess that awareness with their mouths but don't put any effort behind the confession.

The dilemma arises from the myths that surround legal business development. From law schools that never even hint that lawyers will need to bring in business to the lore that surrounds what it takes to grow a lucrative book of business, lawyers are swimming in deep waters full of unrecognized myths. Lawyers buy into these myths and become numb to their potential as rainmakers. Without exposing those myths, all of the "how to" information is likely to fail... And when rainmaking fails, practices shrivel and livelihoods end.

Fortunately, the solution to the dilemma is simple: Expose the myths for what they are. Counter the myths with reality. Doing so tills the soil and makes it possible to implement the "how to" information effectively.

Chapter 2

Solving the Rainmaker's Dilemma

Most lawyers enter private practice with some distaste for marketing and business development. That attitude is fostered (if not engendered) by law schools that fail to mention, much less teach, the reality that a practice requires clients and that client acquisition calls for something more than hanging a literal or metaphorical shingle.

Once a lawyer comes to accept that business development is necessary, new attitudes crop up and create discomfort. Marketing is often cast as unprofessional and possibly even unethical. No lawyer wants to be labeled an ambulance chaser. Some lawyers are so repelled by the fear of appearing pushy, obnoxious, or desperate—or feeling any of those emotions—that they go for the most passive business development activities, not realizing that passivity generally doesn't translate to business. Others get stuck in the planning phase of business development, always on the edge of moving forward, but not quite getting off the starting block.

When a lawyer is galvanized into action by the inability to meet payroll or concerns about career advancement (or job retention), passive pursuit of business all too often gives way to frantic activity without a clear plan in place. Without a cohesive strategy, random actions yield random results. Lawyers mistake luck for skill and continue with efforts that are not well calculated to meet practice growth objectives. Unexamined myths block success, and failure confirms a lawyer's fear: *This is too hard. I figured it wouldn't work. I'm not cut out to be a rainmaker. I'm not good enough.* This is the cycle of business development failure, and exit requires new insight.

The Cycle of Business Development Failure

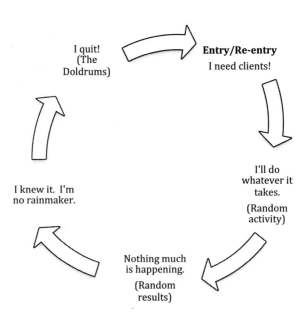

I quit!
(The Doldrums)

Entry/Re-entry
I need clients!

I'll do whatever it takes.
(Random activity)

I knew it. I'm no rainmaker.

Nothing much is happening.
(Random results)

This cycle is infected by two myths:

1. Any rainmaker activity, even if random and not coordinated in a specific business development plan, will generate desired results; and

2. Lack of success resulting from random activity proves that success is impossible.

These two myths, more than anything else, are responsible for lawyers' failure to succeed in business development.

Through business development training, lawyers may acquire rainmaking skills and bring in business. Success tends to breed confidence, and lawyers who experience enough success may overcome the myths with action. But when one setback follows another, unexamined myths begin to whisper and undermine confidence. Although a lack of knowledge or understanding about business development skills may be to blame for the failure to build a book of business, the truth is that rainmaking myths are the silent practice killers.

Rainmaking myths tend to fall into four categories:

- **Necessity**—Myths about the need for business development activity

- **Urgency**—Myths about the urgency or timing of business development activity

- **Mechanics**—Myths about the skills to be mastered for rainmaking success

- **Beliefs**—Myths about the beliefs that strengthen (or weaken) the ability to build a book of business

You may remember these myths with the acronym NUMB. Lawyers who buy into any of these categories of myths tend to become numb to the opportunities that exist for business development success.

Part II of this book explores each of these categories.

Part II

NUMB—Myths that Undermine Would-Be Rainmakers

Chapter 3

N—Necessity

Lawyers are highly skilled at finding evidence to support almost any proposition. Accordingly, no one should be surprised (lawyers least of all) by the justifications for not engaging in business development. The Necessity and Urgency myths are usually specific to lawyers in midsized and larger firms, simply because every sole practitioner knows that a consistent client pipeline is nonnegotiable for the survival and success of the practice. Small firm lawyers sometimes fall prey to these myths, but the truth tends to be revealed as soon as financial pressures uncover the myth.

Even among lawyers in larger firms, these myths tend to be fairly short-lived, especially in today's economy. With fewer law firm jobs available and more press about layoffs, lawyers have a hard time ignoring the importance of rainmaking. Nonetheless, myths accepted unconsciously may persist, even if they are easily discarded once examined. That's why recognition of these myths is critical.

I don't need to have my own clients. I don't plan to stay in private practice.

Depending on your objectives (and your willingness to bet your career on achieving those objectives), you may find that business development is not a high priority for you.

For example, if you want to move into academia, having clients is unimportant for you. However, without stomping on dreams, you must consider the likelihood of achieving those objectives in the reasonably near future. Landing a tenure-track position at a law school has never been a simple endeavor, and given the sharp decline in law school applications since 2010 (a decline that has been in play almost continuously since 2004) and concomitant shrinkage in law school budgets, employment in academia is a certainty for only the narrowest group of applicants. All others will need to have a good backup plan; they may find that law firm practice supplemented by serving as an adjunct professor will serve the desire to teach and to pay their bills.

A more common example is going in-house. Many firms have strong client relationships that may facilitate in-house moves. However, a savvy lawyer will prefer to have her own connections as well. She therefore would be well advised to spend time building relationships with in-house counsel and corporate personnel. Client service and networking are two examples of strategic rainmaker activity that may meet that goal.

All career objectives (whether continuing with a firm, moving to another, starting a new practice, going in-house, moving to academia, taking a government position, or leaving practice altogether in favor of non-legal employment) have one common nucleus: relationships. The priorities for business development and job search are quite similar: lead generation (new contacts or new job opportunities), reputation development, and relationships. Consequently, lawyers who refrain from engaging in business development activity because of their career plans are likely only to shortchange themselves.

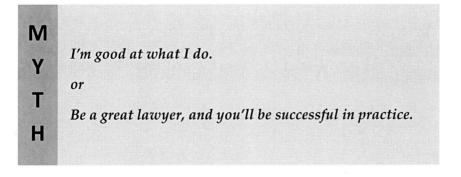

M Y T H

I'm good at what I do.

or

Be a great lawyer, and you'll be successful in practice.

Substantive skill and knowledge are necessary prerequisites for success in practice. Without sufficient skill, you'll likely develop a negative reputation—especially in the Internet age, where clients have so many opportunities to rate lawyers. Although poor practitioners do exist, they often struggle in practice.

But substantive skill by itself is insufficient. Without clients, a lawyer will be unable to develop or exercise substantive skill. The practice of law requires clients. It's like air guitar: without an instrument to play, the exercise of skill is ultimately useless. And history bears out this truth. No one has argued, for example, that the lawyers at now-defunct Dewey LeBoeuf were unskilled. Indeed, the Dewey lawyers were often regarded as top in their field, and about two-thirds of the firm's partnership moved to other firms before the giant's 2012 failure. Dewey, along with more than a handful of other silk stocking law firms and a larger number of smaller firms, went into bankruptcy. On the macro/firm level or the micro/individual level, not having enough clients to fill a practice will always doom that practice to failure regardless of the talent of the lawyers, as demonstrated by the failure of other well-known firms, including Chicago's Altheimer & Gray, Washington, D.C.'s Howrey LLP, and California's Brobeck, Phleger, & Harrison, to name just a few.

A very few practitioners will attract business simply because they are the best of the best. Often known only within their own fields, David Boies might be considered a well-known current example. There are a finite number of lawyers to retain for "bet the company" litigation, or for the most complicated appeal, or the massive deal that needs an extraordinary shepherd to close. These lawyers certainly have the top skills, but they also become, and remain, visible—a key aspect of marketing and business development. They can deliver on the legal needs, and they become positioned as legal glitterati within a narrow field. They won't show up at a local chamber of commerce meeting, and they likely aren't spending time writing a blog, but their speaking engagements, press releases, and books and articles written by and about them keep them in front of their target audiences.

However, even the best lawyers in the world must develop and publicize a professional reputation. Being a highly skilled best-kept secret will not lead to a strong book of business: only a demonstrable chain of good results and relationships with potential clients or referral sources will accomplish that goal. It's the squeaky wheel that gets the grease, and it's the known lawyer who gets the clients.

M **Y** **T** **H**	*I rely on others in my firm to bring in business. I'm a highly skilled lawyer, and that's all that matters for my advancement. There are no adverse career or financial consequences of foregoing business development activity.*

Traditional wisdom holds that law firms are composed of four categories of lawyers:

1. Finders, who are the rainmakers;

2. Minders, who hold management roles such as executive committee members and team leaders;

3. Grinders, who are the worker bees who focus exclusively on cranking out work product for clients; and

4. Binders, who are team-builders who bring the members of the firm together as colleagues.

In today's economy, a lawyer likely doesn't have the luxury of existing in only one dimension of the finder/minder/grinder/ binder quartet. Though exceptions may exist by agreement of the members of a firm, each lawyer is asked to use each of these skills. You need not become a virtuoso in every area, but it's critical to develop some level of skill in each.

A lawyer who insists on remaining in the grinder role is likely to find collegial support as long as there's enough work to go around. However, one of the first signs of financial trouble in a law firm is a decrease in the amount of work to be done, and lawyers often begin hoarding work, either in an effort to stabilize their billable hours or to be the sole point of client contact so that lawyer can "own" the client relationship. Even absent financial pressure, a grinder faces potential financial consequences. Firm compensation structures generally offer some reward to the lawyer who brings in a new client or new matter, and some structures offer multiple earnings for those who bring in significant amounts of work. Career consequences exist as well. Multiple-tier partnerships are generally reluctant to admit a lawyer to equity partnership unless that lawyer is able to contribute to the firm's success by helping with client acquisition. Lawyers may find it difficult, or even impossible, to move from one firm to another without a book of business. And in many firms, leadership positions are awarded to rainmakers and rarely, if ever, to grinders.

Most importantly, as lawyers learned during theGreat Recession layoffs (as well as rumored and expected non-equity partner layoffs that continue), law firm employment is not necessarily secure. A rainmaker will likely be able to move to a new firm before any question of being laid off arises, and rainmakers who choose to remain at a firm will be welcome. After all, it would not be in any firm's best interest to terminate those who contribute to the firm's bottom line with business, especially if that business might be portable.

Meet Rosa

Rosa, a non-equity partner in a large law firm, contacted me because she was consistently busy but had no clients of her own. "My partners love me while I'm doing their work," she complained, "but they shortchange me when it's time to set compensation." Rosa had a conversation with the firm's managing partner, who revealed that she was considered a valuable team player but not a leader because of her lack of initiative in bringing in business to support her own practice and to contribute to the firm's bottom line. She became determined to become a rainmaker, despite her prior confidence that being a service partner would be enough to satisfy her professional and financial goals.

Finally, from a non-economic perspective, being a rainmaker offers control over a practice that is otherwise difficult to attain. Lawyers who rely on others for billable work have little choice in the kind of work they do or the clients for whom they work. The lawyers who land the business, however, get to decide what kind of work to pursue, whether to work with any given client, and even how to manage the relationship. Once you've cleared the hurdle of coming to enjoy business development activity (or at least some aspects of it), you may find that rainmaking offers an unexpected but welcome path to increased professional satisfaction.

| M |
| Y |
| T |
| H |

I'll be able to find a new law firm job without a book of business, no matter my level of seniority.

This might be called a hangover myth: it may once have been true, but its heyday has long since passed. If failing to develop business (or at least make an effort) is a danger sign for retaining employment, is it really such a surprise that it's also a danger sign for gaining employment?

I have already recounted my experience with recruiter after recruiter, all bearish on my chances of securing a new job without a book of business. Those conversations took place in a good economy and a hiring legal job market. Even assuming that a lawyer without a book of business might catch a firm's attention, what do you suppose would be the outcome of two candidates who are roughly equal in legal skill (to the extent that a hiring firm can or does investigate skill), pleasant and collegial, and seemingly vested with good judgment, if one of those two has a book of business? Consider the size of the book: certainly one lawyer with a million-dollar book of business would be likely to beat out a similarly situated lawyer with no clients, but what would you imagine the result would be if one lawyer has a $50,000 book and the other has none? A portable book of business will not always carry the day, but it will be a significant asset in a job search.

Finally, consider this recruiter's comment, reported by former Jones Day partner and noted author Mark Herrmann (now Vice President and Chief Counsel of Litigation at Aon) in an *Above the Law* blog post:

> Law firms buy books of business. Not only that—they buy only past books of business. Nobody buys a story—a promise of future work—these days. Firms buy only your past successes. That's often incredibly stupid, but it's what they do. . . Law firms are even more brutal and Hobbesian today than they were two years ago.... [16]

The post offers reasons why law firms are "stupid" in the way they evaluate a book of business in the course of hiring. And one may rightly be loathe to take career advice from a blog post, without knowing more about the author. However, if this evidence doesn't make you question the validity of the "I can get hired without a book" myth—perhaps you should conduct your own research before deciding to stake your career on this fallacy.

---

[16]   http://abovethelaw.com/2012/05/inside-straight-on-crossing-the-in-house-rubicon-and-law-firm-stupidity/

MYTH

I work with one or two specific partners who are coming closer to retirement age. When they retire, I expect to inherit their book of business.

What looks like security in the form of an inherited book of business may be illusory. Consider the following facts:

- In the absence of a firm-mandated retirement policy, lawyers may not retire at retirement age. Even those who are forced to retire by a firm's policy may take their practice (and their clients) to a new firm unhampered by such rules.

- More and more senior lawyers are choosing to reduce their practice rather than simply retire. That reduced practice may entail fewer clients, fewer hours, or both, but it also means that lawyers are continuing to hold client relationships and the financial rewards of those relationships.

- Clients are more often loyal to individual lawyers than to firms. As a result, although an introduction and show of support from a retiring partner may be enough for a client to stay with you, there's no certainty. At a minimum, you should work now to build relationships with those clients, so that any anticipated client transfer feels more like a natural shift than a possibly disruptive transition. (And the process of developing relationships is business development!)

- If the clients' loyalty does go to the firm, you're assuming the risk that it may stay there if you choose to shift to a new firm.

- Even assuming you do inherit the partner's book of business and you retain those clients, you'll have a *de facto* ceiling on the value of your book and your income unless you engage in business development to expand those client relationships and develop more business.

It is appealing to envision the development of a book of business as a career-long process of client introduction, followed by client service, followed by client inheritance and introduction to a new generation of lawyers, but that's a risky assumption in today's climate. Given that you'll need to engage in client development activity, why not expand that activity to secure your practice so that you always have a pipeline of business?

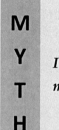

M
Y
T
H

I don't need to do business development activity. If my clients or contact need something, they'll call me.

These beliefs stem from the *Be a great lawyer and the clients will come to you* myth. The problem it creates is simple: if you are not top-of-mind for your clients and contacts, they won't think to call you even if they do need you. What's more, especially if you deal with clients who are not legally sophisticated, they may need you and not even know it.

Meet Jon

Jon handles white-collar criminal defense matters. Most of his clients come through referrals from other lawyers. Far too often, those lawyers fail to appreciate that they need someone who practices in the area every day; they try to handle a matter themselves. After doing the best they can and finding that their best is insufficient, they discover that they need someone who knows the government prosecutors and who can read the subtle signals in government requests. The only way Jon is able to get referrals early in the process—early enough to be of maximum assistance to the client—is to be in frequent contact with the lawyers who send those referrals, either individually or through mass communications such as articles and presentations, so that they think of him as soon as a white collar issue arises.

In an ideal world, your contacts will always think to call you when there's a matter with which you might be able to help. In the real world, your contacts are likely to be so preoccupied with their own concerns that they won't think of you unless you have taken steps to ensure that they know your skills and that you regularly engage with them.

When you engage in a useful way with your contacts (by delivering information that will be beneficial, for example), you raise your profile with those contacts. You may become the go-to person in a particular area of practice by virtue of the relationships you build over time.

Necessity: A Summary

In today's economic climate, every lawyer in private practice must build a self-supporting book of business. If you desire professional security and professional options, becoming a rainmaker is a necessity.

Chapter 4

U—Urgency

Like the Necessity category of myths, larger firm lawyers tend to be more susceptible to accepting as truth the myths surrounding the Urgency (or none) of business development. After all, you're working in a firm, you're keeping reasonably busy, and you can reel off at least a handful of apparently good reasons why, even though you know you'll have to get started with business development someday, that point is in the future, not now.

There are times, especially for larger firm lawyers, when urgency must come from within. External urgency, in the form of a threatened layoff or rejected bid for partnership, will appear only when it's almost too late for you to do what you need to do. Instead, even when no external urgency exists, your drive to build a book of business must provide you with sufficient urgency to get to work.

Likewise, many lawyers believe (or act as if they believe) that there's no urgency to bring in new business when there's plenty of billable work at hand. The inclination is to let up on the business development and focus instead on billable work. The result of that decision is to get trapped in a cycle of not enough work, then frantic business development activity, then enough work, then no business development activity… And repeat.

If business development is something you're willing to do only when push comes to shove—when you can't make payroll, when you're worried about keeping your job or finding a new one, or when you discover that your career advancement depends upon your ability to build a book of business—you've bought into some myths about business development urgency.

Let's review some of the myths that may be keeping you stuck.

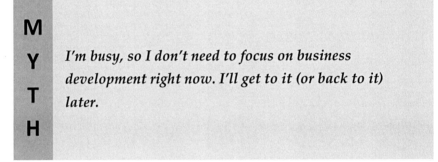

M
Y
T
H

I'm busy, so I don't need to focus on business development right now. I'll get to it (or back to it) later.

Although this myth seems at first blush to be a reasonable accommodation to the press of billable business, buying into it will trap you in the feast/famine cycle, as demonstrated in the following figure.

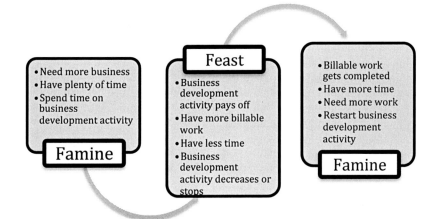

- Need more business
- Have plenty of time
- Spend time on business development activity

Famine

Feast
- Business development activity pays off
- Have more billable work
- Have less time
- Business development activity decreases or stops

- Billable work gets completed
- Have more time
- Need more work
- Restart business development activity

Famine

One of the difficulties inherent in successful business development is that activity cannot stop just because you're busy. The kind and amount of activity may vary, of course, depending on the amount of time you have available, but it's important to remain consistent in key areas. Finding your "Minimum Effective Rainmaker Activity" (MERA) level will allow you to adjust your activity without allowing that activity to grind all the way to a halt. (Visit LegalRainmakerMyths.com to learn more about this concept.)

If you're starting from a feast position, take advantage of the cushion you have. Your current business will allow you the opportunity to plan for longer-term growth of your practice than you would be able to do if you need business immediately.

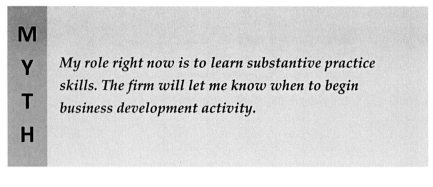

MYTH

My role right now is to learn substantive practice skills. The firm will let me know when to begin business development activity.

Repeat after me: My career is my responsibility.

You cannot abdicate responsibility for managing your career, nor can you expect the firm to act in your best interest unless that happens to coincide with the firm's best interest. You must look out for your own interests.

A law firm is a business and must operate as a business. Each division of the business, meaning each attorney, must perform well without requiring hands-on oversight by the firm's managing personnel.

In the first few years of practice in a larger law firm, associates must focus on learning their area of practice and learning the nuts and bolts of how to practice law. Although law school curricula are changing to include more real-world instruction about what is required to build a practice, every new lawyer goes through a steep learning curve. Even after that initial curve has leveled out a bit, the first few years are, and should be, devoted to achieving technical mastery.

However, the task of becoming a skilled practitioner does not exclude the opportunity to begin engaging in business development activity. Business development tasks fall into one of two camps (or a blend of the two): building substantive skills and building relationships. The balance of those two categories of activity will shift over the career span of a larger firm lawyer, as shown in the following figure:

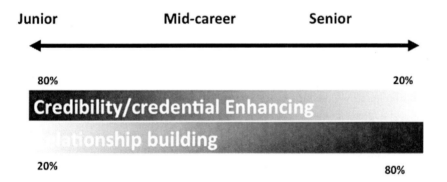

Match Activity Mix to Seniority

Junior   Mid-career   Senior

80%   20%

Credibility/credential Enhancing

lationship building

20%   80%

Associates can engage in many valuable business development activities, including the following:

- Networking internally to build relationships with colleagues and to engage in internal business development;

- Updating a biographical sketch regularly;

- Continuing and building relationships with a network of contacts from law school, college, and other employment;

- Assisting in the substantive work of committees relevant to an area of practice;

- Supporting more senior lawyers with technology;

- Seeking out or creating opportunities to write and speak on substantive topics; and

- Networking and making introductions as appropriate to other lawyers in your firm.

Junior associates do need to focus on developing technical skill, but it is a mistake to allow that focus to eclipse business development activity, especially because some opportunities (such as maintaining law school relationships) may be stunted or even lost if too much time elapses.

Don't expect to become a master rainmaker in your first year of practice. Do recognize the benefits that will accrue if you begin early to grow your network and to develop objective indicia of your professional competence. Business development is like saving for retirement: early investment will compound over time and deliver much better results than a larger investment started later.

M Y T H

I'm a junior attorney. I work in a highly sophisticated area of practice. No one will hire me to handle one of these matters yet, so I should wait to work on business development.

When you buy into this myth, which is similar to the previous myth, you affirm that you are not yet ripe as a practitioner. However, as discussed previously, ripeness is not a black-and-white state but rather one characterized by shades of grey. You will not land a $1M client in your first year of practice, absent truly extraordinary circumstances, but you can engage in business development activity. You will not be the Lone Ranger Super Rainmaker, but you can contribute to your team's business development efforts. You will probably not network among Fortune 50 CEOs, but you can lay the groundwork for a vibrant network of peers and others that will grow as you do.

In 2006, Law.com published an inspirational news story about a lawyer in a highly technical area of practice who did not allow his status as a junior attorney to determine his ability to grow a national presence. [17] Dennis Crouch was a first-year patent associate when he started his blog Patently-O, in which he discussed every patent appeal before the U.S. Court of Appeals for the Federal Circuit. According to the story, his firm landed "less than $1 million" in the blog's first three years. This story is not representative of average results of junior associate business development activity, but it shows what is possible. If the business results don't impress you, it's worth noting that the blog was also helpful in Crouch's move into academia: professional and career advancement also flow from such activity. The moral of the story: no lawyer is too junior to contribute in a meaningful way to business development activity, and doing so will likely advance the lawyer's own interests as well.

Even in a highly sophisticated area of practice, you will find opportunities to deepen your substantive knowledge and skill while adding to your credentials (e.g., writing a blog, helping to organize a CLE program) and to grow valuable relationships. The work you do now can lay the groundwork for additional business development activity as you advance in practice. Small steps taken early in practice can yield significant results over time.

---

[17]   http://www.law.com/jsp/law/careercenter/CareerCenterArticleFriendly.jsp?id =1147251931103

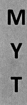

M
Y
T
H

The firm will teach me how to bring in business.

Many firms now offer business development training, which ranges in quality from excellent to barely adequate. If you receive training, view it as a good start but not the final word on what you can do to begin to build your practice.

Learn everything you can and take advantage of firm resources, especially those that will help with necessary research about potential clients and practice areas or opportunities to join organizations and place articles you generate. Recognize, however, that the firm will never be as fully invested in your career as you are. Seek mentors within and outside the firm. Read books and articles about rainmaking, and consider investing in additional training, coaching, or consulting. When you do, you can increase your knowledge, develop contacts, and fill your "business development toolbox" with ideas from a variety of sources. Some firms may even cover or contribute to the costs.

The basics of business development may be simple, but as you explore the scope of resources available, you'll find that every person will bring a slightly different spin to the subject. Some rainmakers are social butterflies who relish any opportunity to connect with a large group of people, and others prefer to meet contacts one-on-one. Some rainmakers speak, others write, and some do both. Even when a lawyer's practice is entirely different from your own, you may pick up a valuable pointer. For example, you can learn something about how to qualify potential clients from a lawyer whose clients come mostly through website contacts, even if your practice is not at all amenable to online prospecting.

Learn everything you can through your firm and through mentors. Even more importantly, if your firm does not offer business development training, do not take that omission as an indication that business development is unimportant to the firm. Remember, you must be in charge of your career and the growth of your practice.

M Y T H

I've pitched business development ideas to the partners on my team (or in my firm), but there's never any movement. There's no point in my continuing to work on this.

Meet Paul

Paul was an ambitious Of Counsel practicing intellectual property litigation in a firm of about 100 lawyers. He was a second-career lawyer with a decade of experience in business and marketing, and Paul was teeming with ideas about how he might connect with new sources of business. He would periodically approach his team leader with ideas, and although the leader never explicitly rejected the ideas, he also never gave Paul the green light to move forward with them. Paul asked for a business development budget and was told none was available to him at his level of practice. He suggested that the firm sponsor an upcoming event and supported that request with data about the other sponsors and likely attendees, but he was told that the firm's sponsorships were awarded based on partner requests only. Paul began to feel stymied, that he had no opportunity or flexibility to try new approaches to business development. He feared that his practice growth would suffer as a result of the firm's reticence. The last time I spoke to Paul, he was gamely attempting to fit his approach to business development in the firm's structure. When I looked him up a year later, he had left that firm.

Clients often tell me about various ways in which their firm, or some lawyers within the firm, stunted their business development efforts, either intentionally or through a lack of attention. If that's your situation you may be facing the difficult decision of whether to stay or attempt a lateral move. However, there are steps you can take to address the situation.

First, get to the basis for the lack of progress. Is the block intentional, and if so, what's the reason? You might consider whether the obstructive lawyers are uncomfortable with marketing in general (and if so, try to uncover the beliefs that are creating rainmaker numbness) or whether they're simply not receptive to the ideas you're pitching. If you find a general recalcitrance to business development activity, you will likely have an uphill battle to change that. You might raise the question of how the firm (or the team) sees its business development opportunities and determine whether the response is proactive or reactive. If the latter, you're unlikely to create a shift on your own.

Second, if the stonewalling seems to be tied to your ideas in particular, consider whether your ideas are significantly different in character than the current activity. For example, have you suggested jumping into social media despite the fact that the firm has only a brochure-style website and no other virtual presence? Have you recommended a shift in the kind of client that firm might seek or a new strategy? If your ideas are out of step with the firm's (or team's) personality, you'll probably find a great deal of resistance.

In either instance, you must evaluate the following questions:

- Can you be successful by adopting the firm's approach to business development (or its decision to avoid that activity)?

- Can you suggest an experiment that would employ a low-risk, limited version of your idea to test it? (See Peter Sims' Little Bets for ideas on how to do this, and think critically about what parameters to use to ensure a fair test.)

- Can you implement your ideas without involving the firm or the team as a whole (for example, a newsletter for your clients rather than for all of the firm's clients)?

- Are you willing to accept the limitations placed by the firm's (or team's) attitude toward business development or its strategy?

Urgency: A Summary

At certain times in your career, you may experience external urgency to engage in business development activity and to build a book of business. However, just as the slow and steady turtle wins the race in children's fables, lawyers who heed an internal call to grow a practice are more likely to engage in the consistent and persistent activity necessary to become a successful rainmaker.

Chapter 5

M—Mechanics

Not all lawyers buy into myths about the necessity or urgency of business development. Sole practitioners generally have no illusions about the need to establish a consistent pipeline of new business or the need to engage in business development activities at every point in practice. For solos, the challenge tends to come in the form of the feast/famine cycle—but those who buy into the myth that they can pause rainmaking activity simply because they have more than enough billable work often become *former* sole practitioners.

Almost every lawyer, however, falls under the shadow of at least one myth concerning the mechanics of business development. Many resources describe what steps to take and how to take them to build a book of business, but lawyers may overlook the details of those steps and then wonder why the steps that seem so simple aren't working. Other times, lawyers understand the individual steps but have not succeeded in ordering the steps in the context of a cohesive plan of action.

Few lawyers have had formal education in even the basics of marketing or business development. Time is often a concern, and as a result lawyers frequently get only "catch as catch can" self-education, piecemeal education through mentors, or high-level formal training that does not dig into specific "how to" details. Myths about how to conduct business development activity flourish as a result.

Many myths exist about how to bring in new business. Accordingly, the Mechanics myths are subdivided into four subcategories:

1. Foundational myths about business development in general

2. Myths about networking and relationship-building

3. Myths about self-presentation and talking about your practice

4. Myths about asking for the business

Foundational Myths

M Y T H	*New business means new clients. I need to convert strangers into client.*

In this myth lies a grain of truth, but that grain is far outweighed by the fallacy surrounding it.

In most practices, the bulk of business will come through some kind of personal contact. For instance, your clients and former clients may give you new business. Other professionals, your family members, or your friends may refer business to you. Although the prospective client is a stranger to you, the shared connection inspires confidence. (That does not mean, of course, that every referral leads to business.) Contacts you meet through serving on boards or working in association committees may hire you. The list goes on and on.

Bob Burg, author of the must-read *Endless Referrals* and co-author with John David Mann of *The Go-Giver,* has formulated the Golden Rule of Networking: "All things being equal, people will do business with, and refer business to, those people they know, like and trust." For bet-the-company matters, a client may approach a lawyer known only by reputation. For more routine matters, and even for extraordinary matters, clients frequently tend to come through personal contact of some sort.

Accordingly, rather than thinking of business development as the process of meeting strangers and getting business from them, think of it as the process of turning strangers into contacts, contacts into warm contacts, and warm contacts into business.

In some practices, this concept varies slightly because of the nature of the practice. When a legal need is especially urgent, a client may not pause to ask for referrals. Likewise, a client may poll friends and colleagues for suggestions about a lawyer and come up empty. In either of these instances, the stranger-to-business path is likely. These practices tend to reach individual clients, especially for personal injury, criminal matters, bankruptcy, and (to a lesser degree) family law matters. Even in these practice areas, however, a referral or an inquiry from even a tenuous contact is likely to carry more weight than a cold communication.

As Jim Hassett, author of *Legal Business Development Quick Reference Guide*, has observed, "[F]inding new clients is the hardest work you can do in a suit." That does not mean it's impossible or even unlikely; it simply means that you will be well-advised to put your emphasis on activities that decrease the need to speed the path from stranger to client.

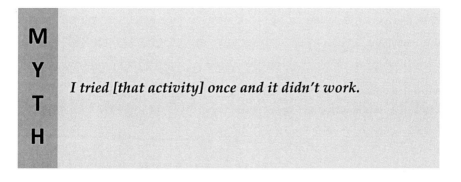

M Y T H

I tried [that activity] once and it didn't work.

Very few business development activities are "one and done" undertakings. In essence, each activity that builds your reputation and credibility, each activity that develops your network and relationships, and each activity that's designed to help you meet new potential clients and referral sources must be performed more than once. It seems obvious, but disregarding this rule is a common trap.

Rainmaking activities require persistence and consistency. Time and repeated exposures make an impact, while a one-off could be simply a fluke. For example, while one article may be helpful to create perceived knowledge and skill in practice, a string of six articles is much more helpful. This principle is even more critical when it comes to making an impression on people: studies show that making an impression calls for seven to nine interactions. (That rule explains why the same advertising repeats over and over: what you don't spot on first glance you may begin to notice after several repetitions.)

Because of variation in skill, exposure, practice area, personality, and many other factors, it's difficult to suggest how many times you should engage in a business development activity before deciding if it does or doesn't work. Generally speaking, allow three repetitions before you do an initial assessment of results (barring unusual circumstances) and six repetitions before you perform any kind of results analysis.

M
Y   *Potential clients and referral sources care about my*
T   *substantive knowledge. How my marketing materials*
         look is not important.
H

If you must choose between substantive knowledge and a good appearance for your website, your business card, or your marketing materials folder, of course you should choose substantive knowledge. But you are not required to choose. With today's technology, you can (and must) design materials that are professional and polished. Otherwise, thanks to shorter attention spans, an unattractive presentation means that you may never have the opportunity to make an impression with your substantive material.

If you work in a law firm with a marketing or business development team, consult with them about how to put together branded and attractive materials. In most cases, you will learn that you'll receive resources such as a template that you can use for reprinting articles and a branded folder.

If you do not have access to a marketing team, consider hiring a graphic designer to create a few items you can use to create professional materials. With only a few simple pieces, such as firm-branded document templates and a sticker for use on folders, you'll be able to create an appealing product to leave with your contacts and clients. Do not conclude that you need an expensive logo or that you should purchase branded pens, coffee cups, and the like. Put your money into creating an attractive presentation of your firm name, using colors that support your branding, and make sure that your online and offline materials are consistent.

Finally, when you are preparing marketing materials, use good quality paper (28-pound paper or heavier stock) and ensure that the overall look and feel of your materials matches the quality of your presentation.

**M
Y
T
H**

All of the lawyers in my practice area are the same.

At first blush, this may be true. You most likely have the same education and similar experience (though the depth of that experience may differ), and most lawyers would say that they are strategic, good listeners, responsive, and smart. Fair enough.

Your task is to dig deeper and find what sets you apart from others in your practice so that your potential clients and referral sources know what makes you the best lawyer for their specific needs. Without a clear point of differentiation, you are simply one of many fungible lawyers, which makes your business development job more difficult.

When searching for what makes you different, consider these examples:

- Does (or should) your practice focus on some subset of clients or issues? For example, you might be an employment attorney who focuses on the food service industry.

- Do you have previous experience or education that is particularly relevant to your practice? For example, if you do white collar defense and you previously prosecuted such cases with the Department of Justice, that insight will distinguish you from other defense attorneys.

- Do you approach your cases in an unusual way? For example, you might offer a collaborative approach. In some practice areas, flat fee billing or a retainer engagement would be a distinctive form of practice.

- What skills or resources do you have that benefit your clients? Consider fluency in a foreign language, a wide network of advisors and service providers you can refer to your clients, or a familiarity with a foreign legal system that's relevant to your practice.

When you determine what sets you apart from others who practice in the area of law that you do, you lay the groundwork for business development activity that is both distinctive and appealing. But remember: the touchstone of these points of distinction must be usefulness to your clients. You should not market based on your skill in rock-climbing, because it will not benefit clients—unless you have a niche practice in representing individuals who suffered injury on a rock climb and now seek to sue an expedition leader.

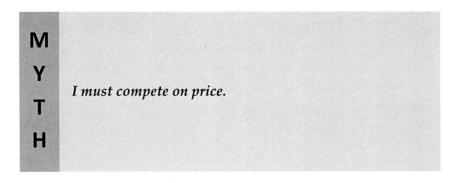

M
Y
T
H

I must compete on price.

If you believe that you are like every other lawyer in your area of practice, then you likely will also believe that you must compete on price. If your practice is completely fungible, price is one of a few ways to set it apart. However, as you find points of distinction that set you apart from other lawyers, you will also free yourself from price competition.

If you serve a niche group of clients, if your practice focuses on one specific issue and you have an excellent track record on that issue, or if you have shaped your practice to meet your clients' needs in some specific and identifiable way, that point of distinction substitutes for price-based competition. And when the differentiating factor is sufficiently appealing to your clients, you may even be able to charge a premium.

M
Y
T
H

I don't need to track my results. I know what's working.

Having some sense of which business development activities are profitable is extremely important as you determine whether to discontinue or to increase your involvement with that activity. Unfortunately, an informal, memory-based, qualitative system for tracking results in not sufficient. Memories fade and may be inaccurate. Just as mental tracking is unreliable for balancing a checkbook, it is insufficient for making decisions about business development activity.

Every lawyer must have a client intake routine that includes determining how that client became aware of you and your practice. Consider incorporating into your client intake form a question that asks, "How did you find out about me/this firm?" If you are working in a larger firm that does not use intake forms, consider creating your own form that requests this information and gathers information about how and when a client wants to be contacted, who else should be kept apprised of the matter's progress, and other information that will help you deliver better client service.

Remember this insight from business performance improvement expert Dr. H. James Harrington:

> Measurement is the first step that leads to control and eventually to improvement. If you can't measure something, you can't understand it. If you can't understand it, you can't control it. If you can't control it, you can't improve it.

Networking and Relationship Development Myths

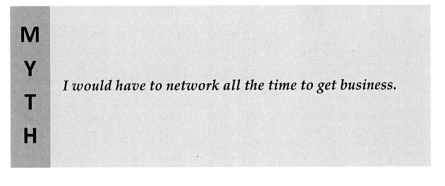

M
Y
T
H

I would have to network all the time to get business.

As already discussed, relationships are important for business development. However, as with any other activity, effective networking is strategic networking. Many lawyers are exhausted by the mere thought of attending gatherings on a daily basis or meeting people with the hope (but not grounded expectation) that some potential exists for landing new business as a result.

More appealing *and* more productive is the process of deciding what kind of people you'd like to meet, determining where those people spend time, and then attending those meetings or events. Business usually results, if at all, from consistent networking that yields relationships, and accordingly your time is better spent focused on two or three groups than rushing to every possible forum for meeting valuable contacts.

Here, perhaps more than any other place in business development, you must know yourself. If you're an introvert and going to large events exhausts you, you should plan to spend most of your time networking one-on-one or in small groups with strategically selected contacts, as well as limiting the frequency of meetings. If, however, you're an extrovert who loves spending time with people, you may choose to spend more time networking, perhaps in larger groups.

You must network one way or another to build your business. However, you need not be a networker extraordinaire to succeed in business development.

> **M**
> **Y**   *Building relationships is nice, but it isn't required for*
> **T**   *business development.*
> **H**

When you are interested in the people you meet and when you make personal connections with them, you're laying the groundwork for a relationship that may, at some point, lead to business. Regardless of your practice area, every relationship you have or develop is an opportunity to grow your book of business. If you are not interested in getting to know people, you will find business development to be a difficult task.

Consider this non-legal example of the benefit of establishing some connection before attempting to move into a business conversation.

I once spent nearly two hours sitting at an airport gate, about five feet behind a stand with Delta American Express card representatives. You've probably seen these stands: a table to the side of the concourse, with various promotional freebies, application forms neatly stacked, and one or two hawkers, trying desperately to get people to pause and fill out an application.

Wearing noise-canceling headphones drowned out the hawker's calls. But as I sat reading, I noticed that more people than usual were coming up to this table, and they were staying longer than usual to talk with the representative. So I pulled off my headphones and started listening. And I re-learned something useful.

The average hawker bombards passersby with the "great offer" they simply "can't pass up." But this rep focused on individuals and engaged them: "You, miss, in the red shirt! Where are you headed today?"

Some people ignored him, but over and over, people paused, walked over to the stand, and talked with the rep. Some told him about their travel delays. Others told him about the jobs they were traveling for or the family they were leaving behind. Several soldiers told him what it's like to be on leave from duty in the Middle East. And the marketer listened. He asked questions and empathized. He was genuinely present with the people who were talking with him.

After he'd heard some part of their travel story, he'd weave in his offer: "Man, wouldn't you like to get an extra 10,000 miles so you can get back to see her more often?" Sure, the rep was trying to get people to apply for a credit card, but he was doing it by connecting with people, by building a relationship, albeit a brief one. And almost without exception, the people who stopped in front of the display filled out something, whether a credit card application or a Delta mileage program application.

Observing this guy reminded me of a Maya Angelou quote: "I've learned that people will forget what you said, people will forget what you did, but people will never forget how you made them feel." What I saw was the power of listening and genuine, though brief and superficial, connection.

The contrast was clear when the connection-focused rep went on break and another took his place. This hawker didn't engage people. He threw out a few half-hearted pleas: "Sir, don't you want some extra SkyMiles today? It's a great offer! You can't pass it up! Sir, you flyin' Delta today? We're giving away 10,000 SkyMiles free—for nuthin'!" Most people passed right by the table and those who did stop received only the sales pitch. I'd guess this vendor's application completion rate was less than half of the other rep's.

Small or large, connection really does pay. And it doesn't require a tremendous amount of effort. It simply requires genuine presence. A good reminder while waiting in an airport.

How can you apply this insight? Write your website copy or the introduction to an article from your target reader's point of view. When talking with a potential client or referral source, ask questions before you talk about your experience and qualifications. Make it your practice to seek to understand before you seek to be understood. Build relationships: they may help you to grow your practice.

M Y T H	*I need to meet a lot of people to grow my practice.* *or* *Networking doesn't work for me. I meet new people on a regular basis, but it never turns into business.*

Landing new business is a relationship-based endeavor, but meeting people is only the first step in building a relationship. Without appropriate follow-up, meeting people will be ineffective, whether you meet only a few or many people in any given period of time.

Your success will depend on your ability to make a strategic determination of which of the people you meet are most likely to yield business, either directly or through referrals. Having identified those people, you must find ways to follow up and build relationships with them. Maintain a short list of the contacts with whom you'd like to develop a closer connection and work toward doing so.

If you make it a goal to meet large numbers of people, you'll increase your network and you may be more likely to reach through your current contacts to someone you'd like to meet—this is, for instance, the premise of LinkedIn. However, when it comes to developing business, it's the relationship, and not just contacts, that matters most.

M
Y   *Social media and the opportunity to network online*
        means I don't need to spend time meeting people face-
T   *to-face.*
H

Social media can be a terrific way to increase your reach. You can meet and communicate with people from around the world without ever leaving your office. However, social media is best understood as another avenue to meet new contacts and to build relationships before you meet in person. It is unlikely, though not impossible, that you will build a productive relationship through online contact alone.

When you meet a valuable new contact online, look for opportunities to take the connection offline. Will you be attending the same conference? Are you traveling to your contact's region? When you've built a bond online, moving to face-to-face interaction allows you to skip much of the "getting to know you" stage of conversation so that you can move more quickly into deeper conversation.

What if you aren't likely to be in the same geographic location but you'd like to expand the relationship? Consider suggesting a telephone call or video conference. In the appropriate situation, you might even send a coffee shop gift card or a bag of coffee beans and have a virtual meeting over coffee.

Moving from exclusively online contact to real-time one-on-one conversation will help you to enhance the "know, like, and trust" factors that started to bud through your online connections and allow those connections to flower into deeper, more productive business relationships.

Myths about self-presentation and talking about
what you do

M
Y
T
H

I need to lead by sharing my experience and
credentials.

When it comes to networking and talking with potential clients, "I" and "we" become deadly words. While your contacts do want to know about you and your practice, none of that information is meaningful until there's common ground. Build that common ground in business relationships just as you do in other settings: ask questions about your conversational partners and listen to their interests and concerns.

Your best strategy for first meetings and the initial parts of a potential client consultation is to remember that people tend to operate from within a self-interested filter. Absent special circumstances, we perceive input by deciding what it means to us. Talking about your experience and credentials doesn't have much meaning to a listener unless you've already built a context of social or business interest.

Consider this quote credited to Theodore Roosevelt and John Maxwell, among others: "People don't care how much you know until they know how much you care."

Instead of leading with your own information, ask questions. Learn about the person with whom you are talking. Explore their interests. You are more likely to have an interesting and productive conversation, and by learning about the other person before you start speaking, you will know how to frame what you do say and to meet your conversational partner where they are, not where you are.

Note that this principle is also true in writing, for example on your website.

M
Y   *Legal jargon makes me sound smart and*
T   *knowledgeable.*
H

Language communicates. In an appropriate audience, legal jargon makes a connection and indicates that you and your audience speak the same language. With those who are not legally sophisticated or are unfamiliar with your area of practice, however, jargon erects a wall that will separate you from your audience. Those who do not understand jargon will stop listening and communication will stop. You will not win friends or business by making your listener feel stupid.

When you speak or write, use language and examples that will connect with your audience. For example, unless you are certain that your audience will understand clearly, use ordinary words to describe the tax consequences of selling one property and investing the proceeds in another rather than using the legal jargon shorthand of "a Section 1031 exchange or Starker exchange."

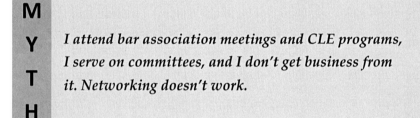

M
Y   *I attend bar association meetings and CLE programs,*
     I serve on committees, and I don't get business from
T   *it. Networking doesn't work.*
H

Consider these two questions:

- Are your ideal clients lawyers?

- Are your key referral sources lawyers?

Unless you answered yes to at least one of those questions, do not consider networking with lawyers to be business development networking. Consider it to be a professional development activity: you may have opportunities to develop your substantive skills and knowledge. But if lawyers are not your ideal client or a key source of referrals for you, networking with lawyers is unlikely to lead to business.

M **Y** **T** **H**	*All my contacts know what I do and can refer business to me.*

Some of your contacts will know what you do well enough to make good referrals to you, but the majority of your contacts will not understand the scope of your practice well enough to do so. For example, if you do "family law," does that mean you handle divorce and custody, adoption, elder law, and other issues that families must address? Complexity increases as the scope and sophistication of your practice increases.

Your contacts will not be able to make appropriate referrals to you unless they know exactly what you do and how to recognize an issue that you address. If you have any doubt, err on the side of seeking to educate your contacts about your practice.

Consider creating a one-page document that outlines your practice, provides examples of issues that you address, and lists the characteristics of a good referral. In appropriate situations (meaning, for example, in conversations with potential referral sources or close friends, but probably not in a networking setting with strangers), share that document. You will get better referrals, which benefits you as well as the person making the referral.

Myths about asking for business

M Y T H

I don't need to ask for business. It's obvious that I want the business.

Leave nothing to chance in your business development conversations. If you don't ask for the business in some way, your contact may think that you're simply giving some helpful suggestions, that you're willing to do the work at no charge, or that you're too busy to handle their matter. You could come across as being uninterested or unresponsive. You may even unintentionally convey the message that you don't like your contact. At a minimum, you will seem unenthusiastic, and your contact may prefer to hire or refer to a lawyer who is enthusiastic about the work and the client.

You must ask for business.

How you ask, however, will vary based on the specific situation. Consider whether you can ethically ask for business, and then find the language that is appropriate in context. Your "ask" may be as explicit as, "May I handle this for you?" or implicit as in, "I'd like to help you with this." In most cases, your request will be somewhere along this continuum.

Know the applicable ethics rules, know your contact, and know the context in which you'll ask for business. Never close a conversation with a potential client or referral source without asking for the business.

Mechanics: A Summary

Few law schools teach the mechanics of business development. Most lawyers learn about how to build a book of business based on articles, training, and suggestions from and observations of mentors. While each of these sources of knowledge can offer useful insight, lawyers must construct a unified understanding of how and when each method of business development should be used as a part of a cohesive, strategic rainmaking plan. Buying into myths about the mechanics of business development increases the likelihood that you will struggle as you work to grow a clientele, so spend some time questioning what you think you know about how to build a practice.

Chapter 6

B—Beliefs

Like the letter "B" in the word "numb," beliefs may be silent yet present. A more insidious reason for lawyers' challenges in business development than misunderstandings about Necessity, Urgency, or Mechanics, Beliefs often go unexpressed and untested. Another way to think about B is that Beliefs are often blind spots, so much so that you are unaware of your beliefs in the same way that you might not see a car in your path.

Thanks to the phenomenon of confirmation bias, we tend to seek out information to support that which we are predisposed to accept as true. In other words, if you hold a belief about business development, not only is it likely that you've never stepped back to question whether your attitude is an opinion or a fact, but it's also likely that you're conscious of information that confirms your belief and you disregard information that conflicts with it.

Myths about business development often implicate beliefs about money, value, and ability. Unless they are brought to light, these beliefs may cause you to make decisions and take actions that are counterproductive. Although an endless number of these myths exist, spawned by life experiences and perceptions, the following are the most common and potentially the most detrimental to growing a book of business.

M
Y *Business development = Sales*
T *Sales = Unprofessional and unethical*
H

For many lawyers, "sales" is a four-letter word. The word may conjure the stereotypical used car salesman ready to unload a lemon simply to make a quick buck. And, of course, no one wants to be a part of that sale—to sell or to buy. No one wants to be (or be thought by others to be) the stereotypical ambulance chaser.

A sale, however, only refers to the exchange of money for a good or service. There's nothing unprofessional or sleazy about that. The distaste we feel for sales comes from how the sale is made, not from the fact of the sale itself.

If you are repelled by unethical business development tactics, you will likely go out of your way to avoid engaging in them yourself. To be certain, start by reading your jurisdiction's ethics rules, and reread them at least annually because rules and commentary may change. In most cases, you will find the rules broad enough to encompass any type of activity you might choose to do. If you have any question, you'll need to find answers before you proceed. This is not the place to hope or assume something is acceptable.

The bigger concern, then, is not about ethics. Rather the concern is about appearance. Does your business development activity look (or feel) pushy? Desperate? Obnoxious? Would someone view the fact or the substance of your business development activity or materials as an indication that your practice is not doing well? Is there anything unprofessional about business development or marketing? These are the real questions.

To get clear answers to these questions (because it's probably no surprise that business development done well is never pushy, desperate, obnoxious, unprofessional, or anything along those lines), let's look at what business development encompasses.

Although the terms "marketing" and "business development" are often used interchangeably, their functions are separate and unique. The process of client acquisition is broken into creating and growing relationships on the one hand and building credentials, credibility, and reputation on the other. Simply put, business development encompasses the former functions and marketing encompasses the latter. Creating written materials such as blogs, articles, and newsletters is marketing, as is branding and strategic planning. Business development includes the process of attending association meetings, perhaps speaking, and following up with contacts. Business development is the one-on-one (or team-on-team) conversation that precedes being retained. Cross-selling and discussing the expansion of the scope of a representation is also business development.

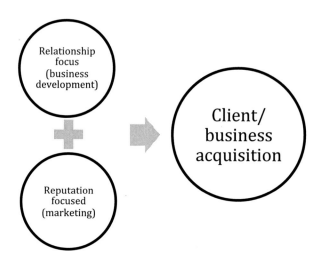

Does the distinction matter? Not really. Consider this: When you approach your business development activity from the perspective of relationship-building and service, you will almost certainly come across positively. Service calls on you to explore the potential client's situation and objectives, to share your skill and experience in the area, perhaps to make some initial suggestions on approach, and to determine whether a good match exists between the potential client's needs and what you have to offer. Business development, at its most successful, is an exploratory conversation. Both sides bring information to the table, and both seek information and a sense of comfort from the other. If there's a match, business results. If not, you have formed a connection that may lead to a referral or work in the future.

If you approach business development from need (as in, *I need this business to make payroll or to make partner*), the lines become blurred. An unspoken self-interest may cloud your ability to explore the potential client's needs or to give a fair evaluation of the matter's merits or your ability to meet the need. The same self-interest may blind (there's that other B again) you to warning signs about the client: hints of an inappropriately demanding or unrealistic outlook, signs of inability or unwillingness to pay your fee, or a fundamental philosophical mismatch. The risk of appearing pushy, obnoxious, or desperate comes into play when your self-interest controls the conversation.

Your approach to business development and marketing will determine whether that activity seems unprofessional, pushy, or desperate. When you come first from an attitude of service (even when you also want the fee or the client relationship) you will put the relationship before the retention. In doing so, you will avoid the risk of feeling aggressive (rather than assertive), too eager (rather than deliberate), or rash. Your prospect will relax and more easily engage in the conversation.

M	*Rainmakers are born, not made.*
Y	*or*
T	*Any failure or rejection proves that I'm not a*
H	*rainmaker.*

According to this myth, unless you have some special predisposition to business development ability, you will be unable to build a book of business. Some evidence is consistent with this belief. According to Dr. Larry Richard, a Director of Hildebrandt Barker Robbins, 20% of lawyers are natural marketers, 55% can learn to be rainmakers, and 25% are "hopeless" at marketing. Richards' research describes various personality traits that rainmakers have and is worth reviewing. (You can find links to articles describing Richards' findings along with other useful information by visiting LegalRainmakingMyths.com.)

The valuable information to be gleaned from Richards' research is that certain traits increase the likelihood of success at rainmaking: creativity, enthusiasm, extroversion, and interactivity. Research by Daniel Pink, author of *To Sell Is Human* (among other books), indicates that ambiverts—those who are not strong extroverts or introverts—actually do better at sales, however, and he identifies characteristics that facilitate sales ability and how to master sales skills.

If you accept that a certain group of people will be unable to become rainmakers, confirmation bias may incline you to conclude that you are a member of that group every time you suffer a business development setback. That conclusion makes it less likely that you will press yourself to excel in business development and, if repeated over time, becomes a self-fulfilling prophecy.

Instead, study the characteristics that tend to indicate success in sales. Work to strengthen the characteristics you have, and explore opportunities to develop those that are lacking. For example, you can learn techniques to improve resilience, which is less common among lawyers than in the general public, and Richards suggests participating in a rainmaker group to lessen the sting of rejection as you see that others suffer rejection and yet continue toward their objectives.

Moreover, educate yourself about business development strategy and tactics and create a structure to maximize the likelihood that you will succeed. Create a board of directors for your business development effort: get help from a variety of professionals, paid and unpaid. Study and practice rainmaking skills, and track the results of your work so that you have hard data rather than impressions that may be colored by your most recent accomplishments or failures.

What if you conclude, and evidence bears out, that you are not cut out to be a rainmaker? In this case, do what you can. Build your skill and reputation through writing and speaking, and work to build a network of contacts who are, or who interact, with your ideal clients. You may not become a top-notch rainmaker, but every lawyer can learn to bring in some business and, for those working in a law firm, to support those who are strong rainmakers.

M
Y   *Business development is harder for me because*
T   *I am _____, and _____ have it easier.*
H

You might complete these blanks with any number of attributes:

- I'm a woman (and men have it easier)

- I'm a man (and women have it easier)

- I'm too young (and older lawyers have it easier)

- I'm too old (and younger lawyers have it easier)

- I'm working in a small firm (and large firm lawyers have it easier)

- I'm working in a large firm (and small firm lawyers have it easier)

- I'm a litigator (and transactional lawyers have it easier)

- I'm a transactional lawyer (and litigators have it easier)

No matter what you believe makes rainmaker activity harder for you and easier for another group, you will be able to find evidence to support your proposition. That's confirmation bias at work. However, if you dig deep, you will find reasons why that evidence doesn't tell the full story.

For example, you might believe that large firm lawyers have it easier. They have larger budgets, a marketing department to help with business development and research, administrative staff to help prepare marketing materials, plus associates and others to shoulder some of the burden of writing articles and preparing presentations. But small firm lawyers have other advantages: decision-making is streamlined, having fewer conflicts opens the pool of potential clients, firms can be more nimble and respond quickly to changing circumstances, and so on. So, who has it easier, lawyers in large firms or lawyers in small firms? Perhaps the conclusion is that neither group has it easier; they simply have it different.

If you hold the belief that some group has an easier time of business development than you do, you will be more likely to spot what makes it difficult for you than what makes it easy. Don't buy into this faulty premise: look for the advantages that you have, not the difficulties.

M **Y** **T** **H**	*There's only one effective way to be a rainmaker.* *or* *I'm doing activity because [name] did and it worked well for that rainmaker.* *or* *I must master all business development skills to succeed as a rainmaker.*

Relationship- and reputation-building are nonnegotiable when it comes to business development, but many paths exist to meet those objectives. For example, the stereotypical rainmaker's relationship-building activity is golf. Not a golfer? Consider inviting contacts to a wine tasting, to fly fish, to train and run a 5K, to take a cooking class—any activity that you might imagine that you and your contacts would enjoy.

Rather than taking on an activity simply because someone you know has been successful with it, choose activities that you enjoy, that you're good at, and that are applicable to your practice and contacts. Imitation may be the sincerest form of flattery, but imitating what allowed someone else to succeed is often a prelude to dissatisfaction and poor results.

Observe what works for others; but leave room for creativity and innovation. When you're able to do things you enjoy and to get business as a result, you'll enjoy the process of building a book of business, you'll be more consistent and persistent, and you'll likely see better results.

M
Y
T
H

I'm getting some results, so I should keep doing what I'm doing.

or

This isn't working, so I'd better stop.

Many variables influence the speed with which you'll see results. Some practices (typically those marked by highly sophisticated work, lower volume, and a higher fee) have a longer sales cycle, meaning that more time is required to see the results from action because clients are less likely to make a quick hiring decision. Other practices have a shorter sales cycle, and so a lack of short-term results is indicative of a problem in the rainmaking plan.

To evaluate your results and determine whether to continue or to stop an activity, you must know three things:

1. The length of your sales cycle;

2. The specific objectives of each activity you've implemented (i.e., not "get business" but "meet John Doe of XYZ Corp., be introduced to the decision maker at XYZ Corp., and find out how they select outside counsel for compliance matters); and

3. The data about the effects of your activity.

Do not mistake luck for skill, and don't judge the failure to land a new client as conclusive proof that you can't ever land the client. Data and context will help you determine whether to continue an activity or to quit.

M Y T H

I engage in business development activity primarily to promote my services.

Promoting your services may be the ultimate objective of your business development activity, but you will have different goals for each of the activities you'll undertake to reach that ultimate objective. For instance, when you're networking, your aim is to become known, liked, and trusted, and to build relationships with potential clients and referral sources. When you're writing or speaking, your goal is to build credentials and a track record that show that you are competent and respected in your field of practice.

Just as you need to examine the overall arc of your results in business development activity before deciding how effective a particular activity is, you need to keep in mind both short-term and long-term goals for your activity. That dual focus will help you to evaluate results and to choose activities based on your objectives.

M Y T H	*I can build my practice without investing much (or any) money.* *or* *I need to invest a lot of money to build my practice.*

The key to business development success is strategy, not investment. However, you must plan to spend both money and time as you seek to grow your book of business. Investments of money might include training and education, entertainment, association memberships, marketing materials, and website or blog design and maintenance. Without these expenditures, you will find it difficult to reach the potential clients and referral sources beneficial for your practice or to create a professional image for your practice.

Beware, however, of the lure of spending large sums of money without a clear reason to expect strong results. Some of the most common expenses that do not garner the desired rewards are search engine optimization, legal directories, and "pay to play" speaking opportunities. Each of these services can be useful, but you must investigate the opportunity and the provider, and make certain that the expected results align with your business development strategy.

If you work in a law firm, find out whether there is a budget for business development activity. If so, use that budget strategically, and keep records so that you can demonstrate the value you received for the money you spent. If no budget is available, or if you're a sole practitioner responsible for setting your own budget, list all the expenses you might incur and then prioritize those expenses based on your business development plan. Doing this exercise is essential even if your firm financially supports rainmaking activity because you may decide to invest personal funds as well. And, with the changing economy and an uncertain future you might decide to become a solo practitioner, at which point setting your own budget will no longer be optional.

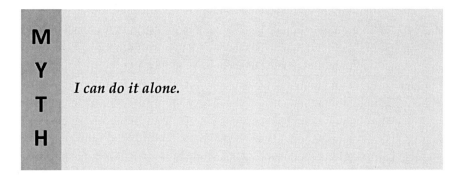

M
Y
T
H

I can do it alone.

You must build your book of business yourself, but you need not do it alone. Look for support in the form of mentors (paid and unpaid), groups of colleagues who are also focused on business development, and educational opportunities. You cannot grow a practice in a vacuum, and as you learn to reach out to your contacts and ask for help in the form of opinions, introductions, or support, you'll find that benefits accrue.

Beliefs: A Summary

Unlike myths about the Necessity, Urgency, and Mechanics of business development, myths that underlie self-defeating beliefs about business development are often difficult to discover without assistance. When you discover the truth that underlies the corrosive Beliefs you have about business development or the blind spots uncovered by exploring these myths, you create the opportunity to act more powerfully to build your practice.

Conclusion of Part II

The number of myths surrounding rainmaking is potentially limitless, but when you recognize that they tend to fall into the "NUMB" categories (Necessity, Urgency, Mechanics, Beliefs) you will be well-positioned to identify new myths as you encounter them.

Of course, identifying myths is only the first step. You must also uncover the related realities and how to use those realities to build your book of business.

Part III of this book provides an overview of business development strategy and tactics. As you read, make a note of anything that strikes you as wrong, infeasible, or impractical; chances are good that underlying those reactions you'll find an as-yet unnoticed myth.

Part III

Rainmaking Strategies and Tactics — A Primer

If you're ready to invigorate your rainmaking activity and to build a full client pipeline and a profitable practice that will carry you through your career regardless of what may happen in the economy, this section of the book will provide an overview of how to do so. For more in-depth information about taking on business development activity, please explore my book *The Reluctant Rainmaker: A Guide for Lawyers Who Hate Selling.*

Identifying the Reluctant Rainmaker

Many lawyers who have bought into myths about business development are what I call "reluctant rainmakers." A reluctant rainmaker is one who knows (or has a sneaking suspicion) that business development is non-negotiable in today's economy, but finds the process distasteful, potentially unprofessional, and difficult to undertake. The good news is that reluctant rainmakers can learn to develop a successful and lucrative practice—and even feel good about the process.

One of the easiest ways to identify a reluctant rainmaker is to listen to lawyers' objections about business development, many of which are based on myths discussed in Part II of this book. When talking with a reluctant rainmaker, I usually hear at least one of the following objections:

- "I didn't become a lawyer so that I could sell stuff. I became a lawyer so I could serve my clients. I'm good at what I do, and that should be enough."

- "I don't want to bother anybody."

- "I don't have time to deal with business development."

- "Marketing is unprofessional. It's icky."

Before developing a business development strategy and outlining the actions you will take to become a legal rainmaker, you must take six steps to overcome business development reluctance. These steps will help you to reinvigorate yourself as a rainmaker—or to get off the starting block if your reluctance has prevented you from engaging in business development thus far.

1. **Identify specifically what about business development makes you uncomfortable.** This reflection isn't simply navel-gazing. Identifying the problem is the only way to discover the solution. If you're concerned about bothering people, for example, you're facing a different situation and you will need a different solution than if you simply don't know how to begin business development. You must get clear on what your specific concerns and objections are so you can figure out how to counter those concerns. Steps two through six of this process will help you.

2. **Consider your attitude about business development.** Many reluctant rainmakers have the uncomfortable sense that business development is simply about money. They think it's about selling a client to raise money to buy a new boat or send children to college, or whatever their financial desires may entail. In this context, sales may feel like something done *to* someone, which raises the concern that business development is underhanded in some way.

   Shift that thinking. Rather than simply thinking about the sale or the money, focus on the service that you're providing your client. The most important thing here is to get out of the mindset that business development is in some way manipulative or dirty. When a contact comes to you with a specific need that you can meet, it is not manipulative to offer that service.

Even business development activity itself can be a service to your current clients. For example, you might work on a substantive committee in an industry organization and learn about new developments in your area of law as a result. You might make contacts that would benefit your current clients. Your clients will never recognize your business development activity as something that benefits them, but you can learn to watch for those opportunities and use what you learn and do in business development on behalf of your current clients.

Review the myths covered in Part II of this book, especially if you recognize that your attitude about business development is holding your back.

3. **Get some help.** Accountability is often challenging for reluctant rainmakers because if you don't really want to engage in business development activity, you may find it hard to get started or to sustain the effort over time. Find a role model or a mentor, someone who can help you with accountability and give you a reality check.

Meet Martin

Martin published three articles over three months in a newspaper and got two new clients from it. He was disappointed with those results. In fact, he was so disappointed that he planned to quit writing the articles. Because I have more experience in client acquisition than he does, I was able to tell him that getting two new clients from an activity as passive as writing three newspaper articles in three months is nothing short of remarkable. With my feedback, Martin knew not to quit, and I was able to make some suggestions that made his writing more effective. A role model or a mentor can help you to shift or tweak what you're doing.

4. **Get educated about business development.** Read books and articles about business development. Get some training. With a little effort, you can get familiar with business development tactics and start implementing them.

5. **Create a cohesive business development plan.** Random activity leads to random results. You certainly don't want random results, so you need to create a plan that will guide your step-by-step process to land new business.

6. **Get active.** At a certain point, action is the only cure for rainmaking reluctance. It can take at least as much energy,

and sometimes even more, to dread an activity than it does to do the activity. Do not allow yourself to fall into the traps of planning in perpetuity or getting overwhelmed by everything you could do to bring in new business. When you have taken action, check your results—without analyzing them to death. There are very few fatal business development mistakes, but inaction is one of them. You must act.

Rainmaking Strategy Development

The rainmaker's pyramid below presents a model for effective business development strategy.

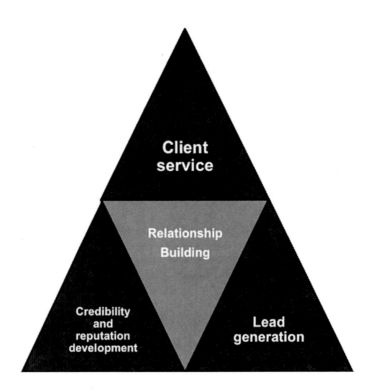

Let's look briefly at each of the four related parts of business development strategy.

Credibility and Reputation Development

It is not enough simply to be good at what you do. You must show other people that you are good at what you do. That is, you must offer objective evidence of your skill. You do that through your credentials, your relevant experience, articles you've written, presentations you've delivered, certifications, and so on. You need to build your reputation and credibility so that someone can search your name and turn up information in your field that demonstrates your competence.

Lead Generation

Lead generation refers to the process of meeting potential clients and referral sources. Sometimes you already have a contact and need to develop the relationship so that the contact becomes a potential client or a potential referral source.

Relationship Building

The center of the rainmaker's pyramid, and the central aspect of business development strategy, addresses growing relationships that lead to client service. Whether you're representing individuals or the biggest companies in the world, you will be hired by people, you will be working with people, you will be referred to others by people, and so you must build relationships.

Client Service

The top triangle of client service should be obvious, but this is a place where sometimes we allow our performance to slide from excellence to good enough. Your client service can affect your repeat business, if your practice is amenable to that, and your referrals. In fact, your client service can also function as marketing itself.

Meet Linda

Linda works with entrepreneurs, and she developed a curriculum for those clients. Her clients went through that curriculum and started talking about it because it was so helpful for them. The curriculum became client service material and business development materials. In fact, new business tracking showed that Linda had acquired a lot of business simply because her clients shared the curriculum with their contacts.

Rainmaker Strategy

The first and most important step for any beginning rainmaker is to create a business development plan. Rather than the plan being an artifact of your planning process or historical document left on a shelf, it is essential that you create your plan and then act on it.

Create Your Business Development Plan

When you understand the model for business development, you're ready to create your business development plan. Visit LegalRainmakingMyths.com to download a template that will help you with this process.

To create your plan you must first ask, What, specifically, do you do in your practice? Be precise. Describe what you do in terms of what you do for your clients. Rather than stating you "do intellectual property," say that you help your clients protect product names and formulas through patent and trademark law. When you take it down to that specific level, you'll present a focused picture that expands your way of thinking and makes it much easier to talk with prospective clients. That specificity will help you with the next steps.

Next, identify your ideal client. Consider the demographics, such as age of the individual or the business, revenue, and kind of industry in which ideal clients work. Defining your ideal client clearly is essential for two reasons.

1. A clear description will help you know where to find those people.

2. A clear description will help you discover who else works with your ideal client and how to reach those people, who in many cases will be your referral sources.

Next, ask yourself what sets you apart from your competitors and other lawyers in your area of practice. This inquiry gets to the heart of what marketing professionals call a Unique Selling Proposition or USP. I prefer to reinterpret USP as your Unique Service Proposition. To find what's unique about you and your practice, consider the following questions:

- What is your experience? How does that benefit your clients?

- What contacts do you have? How do those contacts benefit your clients?

- How do you serve your client in a way that's different from other lawyers? How does that service benefit your clients?

See pages 76-77 above for further discussion on identifying your points of distinction from others in your practice area.

When you define your USP, looking always for the benefit to your clients, you create the basis for your unique rainmaking approaches. One-size-fits-all business development approaches usually are ineffective and harder for reluctant rainmakers to implement. When you know how you're different and how that difference helps your clients, you can capitalize on those distinctions and develop unique rainmaking activities and materials that will set you apart from others in your practice area.

Finally, ask yourself how you can best reach your potential clients and your referral sources. Where do these people or these businesses gather? What do they read? What websites matter to them? It is possible to find a client or a referral source anywhere. In order to use your time most effectively, however, you need to go where there are large numbers of the people or businesses you want to contact. The answers to these questions will help you to determine what groups to explore for networking opportunities, where you might want to speak, and where you might want to publish articles.

These are the high-level questions that will help you to build a business development plan. The template available on

<u>LegalRainmakingMyths.com</u> goes into more detail and helps you to get deeper clarity.

When you go through the process and create a business development plan, you'll set your strategy before you choose your tactics. Two risks become apparent in the planning stages, as illustrated by this quote from Sun Tzu:

Strategy without tactics is the slowest rate to victory.
Tactics without strategy is the noise before defeat.

The first and more common mistake that I see among unsuccessful would-be rainmakers is the failure to design a cohesive plan; the second is too much planning and not enough action.

Implement Your Plan

The tactics needed to implement any business development plan are neither secret nor complicated. The key is to understand the framework for the tactics so that you know how to choose which tactic to use based on your strategy and objectives. This figure sets out that framework:

- Writing and speaking
- Articles and CLE presentations
- Teaching & offering seminars
- Organizational involvement
- Social media (including blogging)
- Newsletters and legal updates
- Networking and following up

Credibility-building activity

Relationship-building activity

The specific activities should come as no surprise. The benefit to this framework lies in understanding the circumstances in which to use each activity. If you need to bring in business right now, focus primarily on the relationship building activities, which put you in touch with the people who will be in a position to hire you or refer business to you. Generally speaking, relationship-building activities produce a quicker yield than writing and speaking. Writing and speaking are terrific ways to get your name into circulation and to build your reputation, but it's unlikely that you will get business directly and immediately from a potential client who reads an article you've written.

If you do not need new business urgently, then I suggest focusing your time on the middle portion of this figure. The middle activities, such as organizational involvement, will lead you to develop relationships and to acquire substantive knowledge at the same time. You may end up writing or speaking as a result, and you will almost always engage in some kind of networking in connection with being an active member of an organization. The caveat is that you must ensure that you're choosing the right organizations. Don't go to bar association meetings and call it business development activity unless your ideal client or referral sources are lawyers.

Specific business development tactics include networking, reaching out to personal contacts, getting involved in organizations, deepening relationships with current clients, and asking for business. You must choose the appropriate tactic to match your strategy and your objectives.

Networking: The Non-Negotiable Activity

You must grow your network and to use that network appropriately. In fact, no matter what else you do, you will find some form of networking to be a key component of your business development plan. The question, however, is how to build and use your network effectively.

The first step, of course, is to choose the right gathering based on the identification of your ideal clients and referral sources. Next, before you attend a meeting, set your goals. Perhaps you would like to meet specific people, or you would prefer to have in-depth conversations with just a few people. Perhaps your style might be better suited to talking with many people at the meeting and then culling down to the most interesting and relevant people for further follow-up.

Any of those goals can be effective for networking, but if you don't know what your goal is, or how it fits into your overall business development plan, then you run the risk of doing random activity that produces random results. Getting random results makes reluctant rainmakers especially say, "I knew it. I'm no good at this." When encountering this problem, you will likely find that the plan or execution is faulty, but with some tweaks it could be successful. If you are uncomfortable with networking, check the resources at <u>LegalRainmakingMyths.com</u> or talk with a mentor, coach, or colleague. Don't suffer alone.

When you go into any kind of meeting where you're going to be introducing yourself, you must have a good introduction that is prepared but not memorized. The purpose of your introduction is to let people know what you do. For the best results, introduce yourself in a way that offers conversational crumbs. This way the person who hears your introduction will have something to latch onto for further conversation. If you go to someone and you say, "Hi, I'm John Doe and I'm with Smith & Jones and I practice criminal law," it doesn't really give a lot for your conversational partner to talk with you about unless they happen to have some familiarity with one of those three pieces of your introduction.

Of the various networking introduction formats, the most effective is the benefits-focused introduction: "I help [*a kind of client*] to [*do whatever it is that you do*] by [*however it is that you do it*] so that my clients can [*get whatever outcome they're looking for*]." For example: "I help pharmaceutical companies with annual revenues in the range of $2 million to get the cash they need by negotiating funding deals so that they can conduct clinical trials of drugs in development." This kind of introduction gives information about you, what you do and what the outcome is for the client, while also providing some nuggets that people can pick up on in conversation to move the conversation forward. Know the components of your introduction, but don't memorize it: most people find it off-putting to be on the receiving end of a rote introduction.

In the course of networking, one of the best things that you can do is to ask a question. Remember that most people are listening through the "What's in it for me?" filter. As they meet others and engage in conversation, they ask themselves questions such as, "What is relevant to me here? What does this person have to do with my business or my personal life? What can I learn here that's important?" When you ask good questions, you immediately become an interesting conversation partner for those you meet. You also find out more about the people with whom you're talking, which helps you to keep the conversation going in a useful and beneficial direction.

Keep notes about the people you meet, when and where you meet, who introduced you, and what you discussed, and any additional notes that may be helpful in further contacts. These notes are helpful when following up. They protect you against the embarrassment of talking with someone who remembers far more about your previous conversations than you do. They will also help you to connect people in your network who don't know one another and should meet. When you make valuable connections for your contacts, you create the perception that you have and share resources. As a result, over time you will find that your contacts will call you when they need some sort of help, and that puts you in the flow of information. It helps you to build relationships. Being a connector is valuable.

Follow Up

Business is obtained through the follow up. After meeting a promising contact, you must follow up with that person, and you must continue following up in the course of building a relationship. If you're not going to follow up with your contacts, don't bother with networking. The harsh truth is that networking without follow-up is useless. Many lawyers struggle with follow-up because it's easy to get busy and miss the window of opportunity. Reluctant rainmakers are generally so relieved to have survived a networking event that the idea of follow-up simply escapes notice. Without follow up, however, your networking is not complete.

Because of the volume of people you meet, and the weight of other commitments, you will most likely choose to engage in selective follow up. If you're only meeting a few people, review your strategy to be sure that there's a good reason that your new contacts are so few. When you meet only a small number of people at a time, you may be able to follow up with everybody. More likely, you will meet more than a handful of people, and so you will need to cull your list to the ones with whom you want to keep in touch. Those are the priority contacts with the greatest likelihood of delivering business to you either directly or by referral. You can follow up with other, less high-value contacts as well, but you will do so on a less frequent and less personal basis.

When you follow up with a contact, start by sharing something relevant to your conversation so that you anchor yourself in your contact's memory. Too often lawyers return from meeting new people with a stack of business cards and good intentions about follow-up activity that soon go by the wayside. If you reach out to new contacts within 24-48 hours of meeting them and anchor yourself, you will establish connections and create follow-up opportunities for yourself.

Follow Up with a Note

Right after you meet someone, especially if it's someone who's particularly interesting to you, contact that person. Send an e-mail or even a handwritten note that identifies where you met and something about your conversation. If you can share a resource relevant to your conversation, do, but even a note by itself is sufficient if delivered soon enough after meeting.

Follow Up with LinkedIn

The next step is to send a LinkedIn request a few days later. (If you are not currently using LinkedIn, start. Now.) When you send a LinkedIn request, be sure to include something relevant to your conversation, or at least identify when and where you met. You have probably received the generic requests that just say, "I'd like to add you to my professional network" or "Good to see you on LinkedIn." Busy people who often meet new contacts are unlikely to remember every person they've met, especially if more than a short time has elapsed between your meeting and the time that you send the request. For now, personalized LinkedIn requests are available only from the desktop web version. Until LinkedIn makes it possible to send a personalized request from the mobile LinkedIn application, you will need to send requests from your computer using the notes that you made immediately after meeting your contact.

The message can be quite simple: "Gerald, I so enjoyed meeting you at the ALVA meeting last Thursday and our conversation about the new entrepreneurship program at the university. I'd like to keep up with you via LinkedIn." That invitation lets the recipient know when and where you met, and it increases the chance that your invitation will be accepted and will lead to further conversation.

After you have made the initial follow-up, you will need to continue to follow up with your high priority contacts. Divide your contact lists into A, B, and C priority lists. The A-level contacts are the most interesting, those who have the most immediate potential for business. Keep in touch with your A list at least every quarter and, depending on your practice and your sales cycle, perhaps more often. To generate ideas for further contacts, set Google Alerts on your top contacts' names, on their business names, and on search terms relevant to their interests. When something interesting comes in, you can call that person and say, "Hey, I see that you received an award for your dedication to the Boys and Girls Club. Congratulations! How's everything going?"

The possibilities for following up with your contacts are nearly endless. Periodically, invite your high-priority contacts to lunch or coffee. Consider recommending books or restaurants, inviting your contacts to a seminar, or noting a special date. You might also watch for opportunities to introduce the members of your network to one another. Whatever methods you use to continue contact with your network, be sure that you design each communication to be of interest to your contact and to further deepen your relationship.

Of course, networking conundrums abound, especially for reluctant rainmakers.

Reaching Out to Personal Contacts

One common issue is inviting a personal contact into a business conversation in an appropriate way. For example, suppose you are attending a dinner party and talking with the spouse of an acquaintance. Through this conversation, you discover that this person has or may have a legal issue that you could address, or you determine that you are potential referral sources for one another. You would not want to start that conversation in the middle of a social gathering. Instead, you can simply suggest (in the moment or in a follow-up communication) that you share some mutual interests concerning a specific business topic and that you would like to get together and explore those interests.

Note that this is not an overture designed to promote your services. It is not a sales call. Your purpose in suggesting a conversation is to investigate the mutual interest and see what opportunities may exist for a business relationship. Make an appointment to meet with this person in your office, their office, or somewhere else outside of the social setting. The benefit to this approach is that you will not put your new acquaintance in an uncomfortable situation. You're suggesting your interest in further business-focused conversation without running any risk of turning a social gathering into a business gathering. You do not want to offend your host or hostess.

Reconnecting with Contacts

Another common question is how to revitalize dormant contacts. We all let contacts go fallow at some point, due to the pressure of other business or simple inattention. The good news is you don't have to start over. You can send an e-mail with a message as simple as, "Dear Anne, it has been quite some time since we were in touch. I realize that I've not been good at keeping up with you, but you crossed my mind the other day, and I would love to check in with you and see how things are going. Do you have time for a phone call or coffee?" Sending an opening email gives your contact a chance to remember who you are and avoids putting anyone on the spot as you might if you place a telephone call with no advance notice. If you do not receive a response, follow up by telephone. You will likely never get a 100% response rate, of course, but if you have had a good connection with someone in the past, you will often find that this is an effective way to revitalize that connection.

Recognize that new contacts will go cold much faster than established contacts. You may be able to refresh a contact that's a few years old if the relationship was deep enough at some point, but you will likely find it difficult to turn new contacts into vibrant relationships if more than six months have passed.

Getting Involved in Organizations

A third common conundrum arises when you've been active in an organization for business development purposes and then discovered that the group isn't the right fit for your objectives. If you find yourself in this situation, check your expectations. If you're expecting to join a group and have it deliver a constant stream of business right away, you will almost certainly be disappointed. Next, check your consistency in attending meetings. If you just attend sporadically, you're unlikely to get good results from it, so attend a string of four to six meetings before you decide the group is not a good fit for you. Finally, check whether you have attended the meetings long enough to know that you won't get results. Relationship-building requires time, so simply going to a single meeting of an organization will not give you enough information about the group, or its members, for you to know whether it's a good fit for you.

If you go through these questions and you find that it really isn't the right group for you, then let the viable contacts you've made know that you've enjoyed the group, but you're moving on. Put them into a follow-up category in your communication routine so that you can stay in touch with them. And then move on to the next organization on your list based on your business development plan. Just don't decide based on one or two poor experiences that you will never succeed in landing business through contacts you meet at an organization.

Deepening Relationship with Existing Clients

Your clients are at the heart of your business development priorities. They are the current fruit of your business development efforts and the seeds for new business. Treat building relationships with your clients with the same importance that you accord their billable work. Bear in mind that every time you talk with a client, even every time you send an e-mail or a letter to a client, you have an opportunity to build or diminish your relationship. Those contacts are opportunities for repeat business, for keeping the business that you have, and for referrals. Don't overlook the importance of providing excellent substantive work and excellent service to your clients and forming solid relationships as you do so. Look for opportunities to meet your clients face-to-face or virtually face-to-face (through Skype or FaceTime, for example) when you can.

Know your clients' business strategies and plans. You are most likely working on only one narrow slice of your client's business or life. Understanding how that slice fits in the whole will be helpful. Doing so will allow you to make recommendations based on the overall context, and you will also have better opportunities to bring information proactively to your clients, even when that information addresses an issue outside the scope of your representation.

Get to know your clients as individuals. This is especially important when working with organizations. Remember that the individuals who are your client contacts in one organization today may move to another entity in the future. When you build individual relationships, you have an opportunity for new business if they should move to another organization. This approach is especially effective for more junior attorneys in law firms. You may not have client contact with C-level corporate representatives, but you will have the chance to meet, and work, with corporate employees on your own peer level. As your career advances they too will advance in seniority, and maintaining your relationship can create wonderful opportunities as time passes.

Be proactive to meet your clients' needs. Through organizational involvement, preparing for speaking, and writing articles and books or book chapters, you may discover information or new developments that are pertinent to your clients. Bring that information to your clients as appropriate. Send the article, invite them to the seminar, or schedule a meeting to discuss new issues. Your clients will never connect this service with business development, but you will at least deliver better client service, and possibly even expand the scope of a current representation, on the basis of what you learn.

Finally, stay in touch with your clients. An update delivered by telephone or in writing on a schedule appropriate to the matter will build the relationship through serving your client well. Be sure that your updates match your clients' preference for frequency and form of communication.

Asking for Business

One of the most important aspects of business development is asking for the business. Without making such a request your contacts may think that you don't want the business or that you're offering to help at no charge. Even in the absence of a specific conversation, you may find it appropriate to let a contact know that you would like to work with them if the opportunity ever arises. While asking for business may not feel comfortable to you, you will find that it can open useful conversation.

Asking for business in the context of conversation with a prospective client is a three-step process.

1. Make sure you actually want to handle this matter and this client.

2. Make sure that you can ethically ask for the business and that it would be appropriate to do so in the context of the

relationship.

3. Find a genuine way to express interest in the client and the matter and request (explicitly or not) to handle the business.

The following figure presents the three questions you must consider in the context of asking for business.

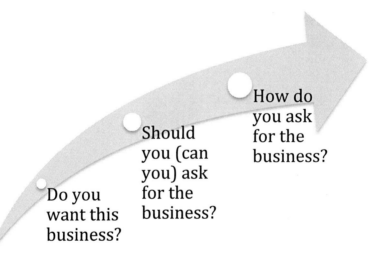

Do you want this business?

Should you (can you) ask for the business?

How do you ask for the business?

Lawyers who are financially strapped often falter on the first two steps, being far too eager to get a client, any client, at any price. Be aware that some clients will cost you (in money, time, energy, or all three) far more than the income they bring. Learn to identify those clients before you take their matters. Develop the discipline of rejecting the work when necessary so that you can avoid the pain of having accepted it. Likewise, know the rules in your jurisdiction about asking for business (as well as all other aspects of business development and marketing) and ensure that you stay well within the bounds.

Making the actual request for the business is comprised of a three-phase continuum as shown:

Listen | Share | Ask

Listen. First, listen and make sure that your prospective client feels heard and that you understand where this client is going and what his or her concerns are. You are not required to let the client ramble on for hours, but remember that you're establishing the basis for your attorney/client relationship even in the initial conversation. Listen for clues about objectives, the perceived issues, the real issues, and any warning signs that you may not want this client or this matter. Ask questions to get the information you need and to demonstrate that you are listening and processing the conversation.

Share. When you have heard enough, then you can share your relevant experience, any approaches that you think that might be helpful for this prospective client, resources, and issues or results that the client may not have considered. You may go back and forth several times between listening and sharing before you ask for the business.

Ask. Asking for business can be especially difficult for reluctant rainmakers who fear that they are being manipulative or mercenary in their efforts to get new business. Review the image in the "ask" panel in the figure above. Think back to a time when you needed help and when you found someone who could assist you: a legal matter, perhaps, or something as simple as finding an accountant to help with your taxes or even a dogsitter to care for your animals so you could visit a sick relative. Remember the feeling of relief when you knew you'd be able to get the help you needed. That's what business development is about.

The language that you will use to ask for business depends entirely on your practice, your clientele, and your own preferences, as well as the specific situation at hand. The request may range from rather oblique ("Would you like me to suggest an approach based on our conversation?") to quite explicit "May I handle this matter for you?"). Regardless of the specific request you make, the language must be genuine and clear.

If you fail to ask for the business, the person with whom you're talking may think that you're simply being helpful or that you're too busy and you don't want the business.

Meet Tom

Tom worked for years to build a business relationship with a high-priority contact. After a personal friendship had developed and Tom saw business go repeatedly to his competitors, he asked his contacts why he never had the opportunity to get the work. Tom was astonished to learn that his friend genuinely believed that he did not want the business because he never asked.

In the context of asking for the business, be prepared to discuss financial arrangements. This is a business conversation, after all, and even if your client doesn't raise the question, you can be sure that it is an important topic.

Ideally, at this point, after you've had a full conversation about the matter, asked for the business, and discussed the financial arrangement, you'll have a new client. Sometimes, perhaps more often than not, the prospective client will not engage you immediately. The way you handle gentle rebuffs and delays in responding can make the difference between getting the business and not. Use open-ended questions to keep the conversation going, and go back to listening. Ask questions designed to get more information so that you can target your comments in a way that will better connect with this prospective client. Get clear on the client's perspective, objectives, assumptions, concerns, and fears, and address them.

You may also invite collaboration, whether as a part of asking for the business or as a part of the representation itself. In the past, clients liked to bring a legal issue to a lawyer, have the lawyer metaphorically take the issue into the back room and deal with it, then return it to the client, all tidy and settled. The trend now, which shows no signs of abating, is that clients want to understand what the issues are, to have a say in the resolution, and in some instances to contribute, or to bring other resources in, to address the matter. Cost plays a large factor here, and by inviting collaboration and discussing finances, you'll uncover any concerns that touch on budget or fee minimization.

Remember that, at its foundation, a consultation is a conversation, not an interview followed by your sales pitch.

Finally, if you don't receive a solid answer to your request, make a "bookend" follow-up appointment. Set a specific date and time to meet with the prospective client again and check in on the decision-making process. Your goal at the end of every conversation is not necessarily to get a yes or no answer: your goal is to know whether this prospective client is interested in at least continuing the conversation. If the client is not willing to commit to a bookend appointment, most likely you will not get the business, even if you have not received a clear rejection.

Measure Your Results

As you implement business development tactics, you must determine whether your actions are effective.

You must measure the results that you see from your business development activity so that you can determine what is and is not effective. Before you can record meaningful measurements, though, you must define your metrics.

If your practice comprises lower fee, higher volume matters and a potential client doesn't need to give tremendous thought to the decision before hiring a lawyer, your practice has a relatively short sale cycle. In that case, new business is an appropriate metric for measuring even relatively short-term results. If your practice has a longer sale cycle, however, it will take longer to develop those relationships and for your potential clients to sign on. While new business is an important metric to track, you must also track whether you're moving your relationships forward in a meaningful way, and whether you're engaging with decision-makers. The appropriate metrics for these practices will depend on the specific situation, so be attentive to indicators that you are making progress toward bringing in business.

For Further Information

Business development strategy and tactics is a substantial topic that cannot be covered fully in this brief discussion. Please visit LegalRainmakingMyths.com for additional resources to continue your rainmaker's journey, including the Law Practice Profitability Audit, a 20-question assessment that will help you to determine where you are in your rainmaking journey and the specific steps you need to take to build a solid book of business.

Julie A. Fleming, principal of Atlanta-based Lex Innova Consulting, helps lawyers worldwide to use innovative and effective measures to build a strong book of business and a lucrative practice. Julie is the author of the Amazon best-seller *The Reluctant Rainmaker: A Guide for Lawyers Who Hate Selling* (2009) and *Seven Foundations of Time Mastery for Attorneys* (2011). Her work has appeared in *The Practical Lawyer* (ALI CLE), *Trial* magazine (American Association for Justice), *The Bencher* (American Inns of Court), *ABA Now* (American Bar Association), and *The Glass Hammer*. Julie presented the Presidential Showcase Program *Seven Secrets Every Lawyer Must Know to Thrive, Even in a Recession* at the 2009 American Bar Association annual meeting and is a frequent speaker for law firms, bar associations, law schools.

Before launching her consulting business, Julie practiced law for over a decade in firms of three to more than 2100 attorneys, focusing her practice on patent litigation. Julie is a Fellow of the American Bar Foundation. Previous American Bar Association appointments include serving as Secretary and Vice Chair of the ABA Section of Science and Technology Law; Editor-in-Chief of The SciTech Lawyer; Chair of the Life Sciences and Physical Sciences Division and Biotechnology Committee; Council member for the Section of Science and Technology Law; member of the Special Committee on Bioethics and the Law. She is currently a member of the ABA Standing Committee on Ethics and Professional Responsibility.

Julie earned her J.D. in 1993 from the Emory University School of Law, her B.S., magna cum laude, in biology in 1998 from Georgia State University, and her B.A. in 1990 from Vanderbilt University, and a certification in leadership coaching from Georgetown University in 2006. She is registered to practice before the United States Patent and Trademark Office and is admitted to the bars of Georgia, the District of Columbia, and Florida.

Contact Julie by telephone to 800.758.6214 (if calling within the United States) or 404.954.2523 (outside the U.S.) or by email to support@LexInnovaConsulting.com.

The days of having a practice supported by being a "great lawyer" are gone forever. In today's economy, every successful private practice lawyer is a rainmaker who has created an effective plan for building a consistent pipeline of new business. Rainmakers harness their unique strengths and perspectives to create a cohesive, strategic, simple-to-implement plan—and they take consistent, focused action on that plan.

However, too many would-be rainmakers fall victim to myths about when, whether, and how they should engage in business development activity. Inside, you will discover the myths that capture aspiring rainmakers and the reality that will unleash your ability to build a profitable book of business.

Julie A. Fleming, principal of Lex Innova Consulting, teaches lawyers to use innovative and effective measures to build a strong book of business and a lucrative practice. A former patent litigator, she is the author of *The Reluctant Rainmaker: A Guide for Lawyers Who Hate Selling* and *Seven Foundations of Time Mastery for Attorneys*.